M000285939

HASIDIC WISDOM

HASIDIC WISDOM

SAYINGS FROM THE JEWISH SAGES

SIMCHA RAZ

translated by
Dov Peretz Elkins and Jonathan Elkins

JASON ARONSON INC.
Northvale, New Jersey
Jerusalem

This book was set in 12 pt. URW Antiqua by Alpha Graphics of Pittsfield, N.H.

10 9 8 7 6 5 4 3 2 1

Library of Congress Cataloging-in-Publication Data
Pitgeme Ḥasidim. English.
    Hasidic wisdom : sayings from the Jewish sages / compiled by
Simcha Raz ; translated by Dov Peretz Elkins and Jonathan Elkins.
        p. cm.
    Includes indexes.
    ISBN 0-7657-9972-3 (alk. paper)
    1. Hasidim—Quotations. 2. Judaism—Quotations, maxims, etc.
I. Raz, Simcha. II. Elkins, Dov Peretz. III. Elkins, Jonathan.
IV. Title.
BM198.P5813   1997
296.8'332—dc21   97-19304

Manufactured in the United States of America. Jason Aronson Inc. offers books and cassettes. For information and catalog write to Jason Aronson Inc., 230 Livingston Street, Northvale, NJ 07647.

CONTENTS

TRANSLATORS PREFACE

May God Who blessed the Patriarchs and Matriarchs of Israel, Avraham and Sarah, Yitzchak and Rivka, Yaakov and Rachel and Leah, bless and protect David Wolf Silverman, Arthur Green, and Yitzchak Buxbaum, who assisted in discovering the true meaning of some of these Hasidic sayings; and Arthur Kurzweil, who appreciates Jewish wisdom and literature, and encouraged the translators to pursue their arduous work; and Simcha Raz, whose devotion to Hasidut, then and now, has made this book possible.

We dedicate our efforts to Hillel and Rachel. Everyone is wrapped in a holy light that shines brightest in our hour of love. (Rabbi Levi Yitzchak of Berditchev) May your glowing devotion join in a brilliant beacon of light shining love over your family, your people, your Maker, and especially, one another.

Dov Peretz Elkins, Princeton, NJ
Jonathan Elkins, Tel Aviv

INTRODUCTION

The Hasidic Movement is a wonderful embodiment of all that is unique and original in the unending Jewish heritage. Its tradition of creativity has yearned relentlessly for expression in word and phrase.

It was the Eighteenth Century, an age of harsh edicts and great torment from without, and anguish and adversity from within, an age that opened up vast horizons, great springs that gushed forth with sweet water.

The age—a time of dismal and stifling reality on the one hand, and on the other, a time of great yearning for a purer, more redemptive existence. In light of those stark contrasts, despite the gaping chasm between them, a great insight spread among the faithful: that the two polar opposites were inherently intertwined, connected by unseen but sturdy channels. The triumph of one of the two aspects signalled the downfall of the other. According to this outlook, the elimination of evil could result in nothing else but the deliverance of the forces of the good and the sublime.

First and foremost, Hasidic doctrine saw the essence and foundation of Godliness in all places. "God's Holy Presence fills the world." Everything is a part of the Godhead, because God is everything: the spiritual and the material, the pure and the impure, the Good Impulse and the Evil Impulse. A constant struggle exists between the two polarities, a struggle that finds expression in the human realm, and, indeed, in all of God's creations: in the sublime and in the base, in the deepest depressions and in the highest heights. Each of these qualities is intermingled with the other, and they mutually support one another. Evil is nothing but the footstool of the Throne of Good. Therefore, it is incumbent upon humankind, a humankind bearing God's image, to participate in the effort to mend and redeem the world, to restore those lonely sparks of light that have gone astray, or that are concealed between the world's broken fragments, or that float aimlessly in the upper realms. Once everything has been restored, these lights will bond together in one glorious brilliance, and with it the Jewish people, the entire universe, and even the Divine Presence Itself.

Human destiny, therefore, is nothing but our ongoing efforts to transcend our existence. Yet these efforts necessitate utter devotion to the Creator, a devotion that carries with it an inner security, an unflappable faith in the victory of good over evil, a reverence born of love, and prayer

PARENTS AND CHILDREN

Rabbi Pinchas of Koretz

One parent can support ten children,
   but ten children cannot support
   one parent.

Rabbi Meir Yechiel Levi of Ostrovtsa

A parent is more devoted to his child
   than a child is to his parent.
Why? Because this trait is passed from
   parent to child, dating back
   to Adam.
Adam was the first to bestow it upon
   his children.
But he could not transmit parental
   devotion because he had no parent.

1

Rabbi Menachem Mendel of Kotzk

Such is the way of the world:
Parents are always troubled by their
    children's sorrows, but children are
    never concerned with their
    parents' misfortunes.
Similarly, God is troubled by our
    sorrows, but we are never
    concerned with the woes of the
    Divine Presence.

Rabbi Nachman of Bratzlav

"Take some of the choice fruits of the
    land." (Genesis 43:11)
The choice fruits are the melodies,[1]
    since there is nothing that sustains
    the soul as the melodies of my
    father's house.

---

1. Play on Hebrew *zimra*, which means both 'choice fruits' and 'melodies.'

Humans and Their Maker

Rabbi Shalom Dov Ber of Lubavitch

Everyone is an "only child" in the eyes
of the Blessed Holy One.

Rabbi Aryeh Leib ben Sarah

Ruler of the Universe!
Give me the strength to commit my fair
share of sins.
Then give me the strength to make
amends for all of those wrongdoings
and to regret them wholeheartedly.

Rabbi Yosef of Brod

Ruler of the Universe!
I admit that I have sinned a great deal
    against You, but have You granted
    me only honey?
I have forgiven You for all of the
    suffering, the hardship, and the
    torment, but You must also
    forgive me.

Rabbi Shneur Zalman of Liadi

Ruler of the Universe!
I want nothing of You, nor do I ask
    anything of You but that You make
    your aid and succor known, so that
    "Every creature will understand
    that You are its Creator, and every
    living being will know that You
    fashioned it."
("Malchuyot" section of High Holiday
    liturgy)

Rabbi Aharon of Karlin

Everything can be taken away from
    me—except for my God,
    in my heart.

Rabbi Shneur Zalman of Liadi

> Sovereign of the Universe:
> I do not fear Your Hell.
> I do not long for Your Heaven.
> And I will gladly pass up Your
>   Celestial Angels.
> Do you know all I truly desire?
> You, only You!

Rabbi Avraham HaMalach

> Ruler of the Universe:
> If for even one moment You were to
>   leave the world devoid of Your
>   influence and care, what good
>   would this world be to us?
> And what good would the World-to-
>   Come be to us?
> What benefit could we derive from the
>   coming of the Messiah or from the
>   resurrection of the dead?
> What pleasure might they bring?
> Why should they come to be at all?

Rabbi Menachem Mendel of Kotzk

> Where can God be found?
> Wherever one lets the Blessed One in.

Rabbi Nachman of Bratzlav

God calls upon all people according to
    their nature:
God calls some with a whisper,
And God calls some with a shout.
It all depends on how far away they are
    from their Creator.

Rabbi Tzadok HaKohen of Lublin

We humans chase over the world to
    find things:
We climb high mountains, we descend
    to the nethermost depths of the sea,
    we trek to the wilderness and to
    the desert.
There is one place where we neglect to
    search—our heart.
But it is there we will find God.

Rabbi Shalom Shachne of Prohobitch

There are those who try to ascend to the
    Heavens to reach the Blessed One.
But I know that no matter where I am—
God will be there as well.

Rabbi Zussya of Anapoli

And what sort of God would the Creator
be if God needed to learn from me
how and why to help?

Rabbi Nachman of Bratzlav

Even in the deep recesses of the
netherworld one can be close
to the Ruler of the Universe!
Because God is there as well.

Rabbi Shalom Shachne of Prohobitch

It is better that we look inside of
ourselves and see what is going on
in here, than to look to the Heavens,
to see what is going on up there.

Rabbi Baruch of Medzibuz

"Blessed is the One who decrees and
upholds." (from the Prayer book)
What does this mean?
The Blessed Holy One decrees an edict,
and upholds those who abide by it.

Rabbi Yitzchak Meir of Ger

It is better that I should perform the will
of God than that God should
perform my will.

Rabbi Menachem Mendel of Kotzk

Can a person really reach the
Heavens in one leap?

Rabbi Naftali of Ropshitz

Wholesomeness is greater than wisdom.
But much wisdom is needed until we
reach the level described in
the Torah:
"You must be wholehearted with
Adonai your God."
(Deuteronomy 18:13)

Rabbi Menachem Mendel of Kotzk

When we open our eyes each morning
and recite the prayer:
"I thank You, O God! . . ."—
It is good to reflect for a while:
Who am "I"? and Who are "You"?

The Seer of Lublin

> "And God had blessed Avraham in all
>   things." (Genesis 24:1)
> Avraham our Father was blessed with
>   an abundance of *all* things.
> Which ones? As it is written, "With *all*
>   your heart and *all* your soul and *all*
>   your might." (from the "Shema"
>   prayer, Deuteronomy 6:5)

Rabbi Menachem Mendel of Vorka

> Rather than tearing one's clothes
>   to arouse the sympathy of other
>   human beings, it is better to rend
>   one's heart and win the mercy
>   of God.

Rabbi Moshe of Kobrin

> When we are not strict when it comes to
>   our dealing with God, then neither
>   is God strict in dealing with us.
> Neither in this world, nor in the World-
>   to-Come.

Rabbi Yehiel Michal of Zlotchov

> The Holiness of the Blessed Holy One
> comes from the sacred authority
> of the People who sanctify God's
> Holy Name.

Rabbi Yehuda Aryeh Leib of Ger

> I am no expert in treasures.
> There is only one treasure that I know
> of, and it has been well-tested:
> As God said: "You shall be my treasured
> possession." (Exodus 19:5)

Rabbi Moshe of Kobrin

> It is not enough that you love God,
> you must strive to have God love
> you as well.

Baal Shem Tov

> Even after one has achieved the
> spirituality of an angel, one must
> still abide by the commandments
> like a simple Jew.

Baal Shem Tov

> A simple wagon driver kissing the
>   fringes of his Tallit is dearer to the
>   Ruler of the Universe than the
>   praise of the Angel Michael.

Rabbi Menachem Mendel of Kotzk

> Whoever does not see God in every
>   place does not see God in any place.

Rabbi Israel of Rozhin

> What is the holy spirit?
> One who has spirituality and has not
>   defiled it.

Rabbi Levi Yitzchak of Berditchev

> We remember everything.
> It is only God that we forget.

Rabbi Nachman of Bratzlav

> God hides
>   so that we will seek.

Rabbi Yechiel Michal of Zlotchov

One who truly loves God
> must account for why God does not
> redeem His children.

Rabbi Aharon of Karlin

Our sages teach us to judge every person
> favorably (cf. Mishnah, *Avot* 1:6)
If this applies to humans, how much
> more so to the Omnipresent!

Rabbi Baruch of Medzibuz

The Blessed Holy One oppresses
> humans until their souls are utterly
> dejected and afterwards says
> "Return unto Me."
How can this be possible?

Rabbi Shlomo of Karlin

"You are children of Adonai your God."
> (Deuteronomy 14:1)
The greatest sin of all is when Jews
> forget that they are the children
> of Royalty.

Baal Shem Tov

> "When you were tired and weary and
>   you did not fear God . . ."
>   (Deuteronomy 25:18)
> A Jew can engage in so much fasting
>   and penance that he becomes tired
>   and weary—and still be far from
>   God-fearing.

Rabbi Yaakov Yitzchak of Pshis'cha

> Why is the name of the Holy Blessed
>   One called "I Am Who I Am"?
>   (Exodus 3:14)
> When one is remorseful and says: "I will
>   be good from now on," the Blessed
>   Holy One responds immediately,
>   saying:
> "'I Am' with you and will immerse you
>   in My Presence."

Rabbi Yehuda Aryeh of Ger

> "You shall be holy people to Me."
>   (Exodus 22:30)
> God has no lack of holy angels on high,
>   yet God desires the holiness of
>   *people*—a holy people.

Rabbi Menachem Mendel of Kotzk

"You shall not make molten gods for
yourselves." (Exodus 34:17)
This means: Do not have an overly rigid
image of God.
That is, do not make God into an idol.

Rabbi Menachem Mendel of Kotzk

"Take these things which I command
you today upon your heart."
(Deuteronomy 6:6)
Let them always rest upon your heart
so that when the right moment
comes, and your heart opens,
they can penetrate immediately.

Rabbi Avraham Yehoshua Heschel of Apt

"And Yaakov awoke from his sleep and
said, 'Surely God is in this place, and
I did not know it!'" (Genesis 28:16)
Meaning, "I didn't know that I could
worship God consciously while
still sleeping."

Rabbi Nachman of Bratzlav

> One must not give in to the Ruler of
> the Universe!

Rabbi Baruch of Medzibuz

> "For God knows the secrets of the
>   heart." (Psalms 44:22)
> The Blessed Holy One knows that which
>   is hidden—even from one's
>   own heart.

Rabbi Menachem Mendel of Kotzk

> "You shall have no foreign god."
>   (Psalms 81:10)
> This means: Do not let God be strange
>   or foreign to you, neither to your
>   heart nor to your soul.

Baal Shem Tov

> "Adonai is your shadow." (Psalms 121:5)
> Just as a shadow copies what you do,
>   so the Blessed Holy One, as it were,
>   copies what you do.

Baal Shem Tov

"Know what is above [from] you."
(Mishnah, *Avot* 2:1)
Know that all that is above—is from you.

Rabbi Menachem Mendel of Kotzk

"All of your deeds shall be for Heaven's
sake." (Mishnah, *Avot* 2:12)
Meaning, even what you do "for the
sake of Heaven"—should also be for
Heaven's sake.

Baal Shem Tov

Those who want to praise—let them
praise the Creator.
And those who want to condemn—let
them condemn themselves.

Rabbi Levi Yitzchak of Berditchev

To the best of my knowledge,
The Blessed One has yet to fulfill his
obligation to a single Jew.

LOVE AND HATE

Baal Shem Tov

If your desire is to be loved—
then love others.

Rabbi Levi Yitzchak of Berditchev

Everyone is wrapped in a holy light,
which shines brightest in our hour
of love.

Rabbi Naftali of Ropshitz

Love is the most reliable cure for
wounds of the soul.

Rabbi Aharon of Karlin

Love is hidden in the recesses of
everyone's heart.
There is no one who has not had at least
an hour of love and yearning.

Rabbi Levi Yitzchak of Berditchev

A person in love is like someone lost at
sea, suspended by a thin thread,
in the midst of a raging storm

Rabbi Naftali of Ropshitz

The sign of true love is forgetfulness.
One forgets oneself and thinks only of
the beloved.

Rabbi Aharon of Starosoli

Until you have experienced "the void"
and become familiar with the
terrible depths of the netherworld,
and until you have suffered the
agonies of heartbreak, you cannot
know love itself.

Rabbi Levi Yitzchak of Berditchev

The power of love is glorious—
it can propel you towards the
throne of Divine Glory.

Rabbi Moshe of Kobrin

Just as one is commanded to be in a
state of happiness, likewise must
one live in love.

Rabbi Menachem Mendel of Kotzk

Love may not be bread to eat,
but it is the wine of life.

Rabbi Nachman of Bratzlav

Love is dependent on the mind.
One's hate swells only when one's mind
is troubled.

Rabbi Menachem Mendel of Kotzk

Not only is one who hates another soul
called wicked—but someone who
hates oneself is also called wicked.

Rabbi Nachman of Bratslav

If there are those who hate you here
below, you can be sure that there
are those who hate you On High
as well.

LOVING THE LAND OF ISRAEL

Rabbi Nachman of Bratzlav

My place is in the Land of Israel.
Whenever I travel, that is the only place
    I go.
Though for now, I am merely a
    shepherd sojourning in Bratslav.

Rabbi Meir Yehiel of Ostrovtsa

"Go forth . . . to the land that I will show
    you." (Genesis 12:1)
The commandment to settle the Land of
    Israel is a great one—so much so
    that it is the first commandment
    ever decreed upon a Jew.

21

Rabbi Yehezkiel Halberstam

Whoever loves the Land of Israel
is likewise loved by the Land.

Rabbi Menachem Mendel of Vitebsk

The Land of Israel is the same as the
Divine Presence Itself.

LOVING THE PEOPLE OF ISRAEL

Baal Shem Tov
___

Loving the people of Israel is the
    equivalent of loving God.
When you love the parents, you also
    love their children.

Baal Shem Tov
___

When one loves Jews, one loves God as
    well, because every Jew shares a
    portion of the Divine.
And we know that when one loves the
    part, it stands to reason that one
    loves the whole.

Rabbi Shneur Zalman of Liadi

The love of Israel is greater even than
the love of God, because even God
loves Israel.
Therefore, whoever loves Israel loves
God's beloved.

Rabbi Levi Yitzchak of Berditchev

Our sages instructed us that
"When judging each and every
individual we must give them the
benefit of the doubt." (cf. Mishnah,
Avot 1:6)
How much more so, then, must you give
the entire People of Israel the
benefit of the doubt.

The Seer of Lublin

Righteous people do not need to
love themselves.
Repentant people cannot
love themselves.
But as for other human beings,
why, everyone must love them.

Rabbi Elimelech of Grodzisk

> Those who devote their life to the
>> Household of Israel are greater than
>> those who devote their life to the
>> Ruler of the Universe alone.
> Just as those who devote their life to a
>> prince prove that their devotion to
>> the Ruler is so great that not only do
>> they devote their life to the Ruler,
>> but to the Ruler's child as well.

Rabbi Shlomo of Karlin

> I wish that I could love the most
>> righteous person in Israel
>> as much as the Blessed Holy One
>> loves the most evil person in Israel.

Rabbi Naftali of Ropshitz

> I wish that, in my next life, I would be a
>> cow and that a Jew would come and
>> milk me to regain the strength to
>> worship God.

Rabbi Yisrael of Kozhnitz

When all of the People of Israel clasp
hands, then all of the hands shall
join together like one great hand
that touches the Throne of Glory.

DECEPTION

Rabbi Noah of Lechovitz

The Creator cannot be deceived.
Nor can a wise person be deceived.
The community cannot be deceived—
    they are not fools.
It is thus possible to deceive only
    oneself, and what wisdom is there
    in deceiving such a fool?

Rabbi Menachem Mendel of Vorki

The law stipulates: "One should not
    wrong one's neighbor."
    (Leviticus 25:14)
But one must go beyond the letter of the
    Law, and not wrong oneself.

Rabbi Mordechai Yosef Leiner of Ishbitz

Beware of two things:
Cheating yourself and mimicking
   someone else.

Rabbi Yisrael of Kozhnitz

It is easier not to torment yourself
   and deceive someone else
   than it is to torment and
   deceive yourself.

Rabbi Yehezkiel of Shinova

I despise gold-plated jewelry,
   for it combines both falsehood
   and pride.

Rabbi Simcha Bunam of Pshis'cha

Let the heart and the mind always
   be congruent.

Rabbi Shalom Dov Ber of Lubavitch

Not everyone who gets emotional is
   necessarily someone with feelings.

Rabbi Yisrael of Kozhnitz

> I prefer a scoundrel who pretends to
> suffer all the time to an ascetic
> who fasts often and boasts about
> his deeds.

Rabbi Shlomo of Radzimin

> A rich person who praises poverty
> or brags about suffering
> is nothing but a scoundrel.

Rabbi Menachem Mendel of Kotzk

> One who lets out even a quiet sigh
> that does not come from the depths
> of the heart has committed fraud.

Rabbi Naftali of Ropshitz

> "You shall not steal." (Exodus 20:13)
> I heard ten different interpretations and
> analyses of this verse from the
> Torah, until I almost forgot that
> there was one additional
> interpretation: and that is:
> Do not steal!

Rabbi Menachem Mendel of Kotzk

"You shall not steal." (Exodus 20:13)
This command means not only that you
    should not steal.
It also means that you should not be
    a thief.

Rabbi Menachem Mendel of Kotzk

There are those who go about with the
    seven sins in their heart but cover
    their potbellies with a few pages of
    the Talmud.

Rabbi Baruch of Medzibuz

We have learned that even the criminals
    of Israel are as full of good deeds
    as a pomegranate is with seeds.
It stands to reason, then, that even one
    who is as full of good deeds as a
    pomegranate is with seeds . . . can
    be a criminal!

Rabbi Yitzchak Meir of Ger

A thief has the right to steal only that
which he is lacking.
One who wishes to deceive other people
surely lacks wisdom.

Light and Darkness

Rabbi Arieh Leib Alter of Ger

One can snuff out a candle's flame,
   but the essence of that light cannot
   be extinguished.

Rabbi Tzadok HaKohen of Lublin

Just as darkness is often hidden behind
   light, so does light hide
   behind darkness.

Rabbi Yosef Yitzchak of Lubavitch

One cannot drive away darkness with
   a rod.

Rabbi Shalom Dov Ber of Lubavitch

Even the brightest night—
is still night.

FAITH

Rabbi Yaakov of Radzimin

If one believes in the lovingkindness
of the Creator—then there are
no questions.
And if one does not believe—
then there are no answers.

Rabbi Mordechai of Lechovitz

Without the Blessed Holy One, it would
even be impossible to cross the
threshold of one's own house.
But with the Blessed Holy One, it is
possible to split the entire sea.

Baal Shem Tov

Faith . . . is the foundation of everything.

Rabbi Nachman of Bratzlav

The essence of faith lies in the power of
the imagination.
Because that which the mind can
comprehend can no longer be an
object of faith.

Rabbi Menachem Mendel of Kotzk

One who believes in miracles is nothing
but a fool.
And one who does not believe that
saints can perform miracles is
nothing but a heretic.

Rabbi Menachem Mendel of Kotzk

Faith is clearer than vision.

Rabbi Moshe Teitelbaum

Faith is the key to healing.

Rabbi Nachman of Bratzlav

The soul receives its inner light
from faith.

Rabbi Menachem Mendel of Vitebsk

Belief in God purifies the soul.
Faith in the wise purifies the body.

Rabbi Nachman of Bratzlav

One's faith is renewed on a daily basis.

Rabbi Moshe of Kobrin

When suffering, one should not say,
"It is bad."
Because nothing that God does is bad.
Rather, one should say, "It is bitter."
Because bitter pills are among the
best cures.

Baal Shem Tov

The worst punishment one can mete
out is to take away someone's Faith.

Rabbi Menachem Mendel of Kotzk

"And he trusted in God, and God
merited him for it." (Genesis 15:6)
The strength and ability to believe in
God was planted in Avraham our
Father, and Avraham considered it
an act of God's lovingkindness,
which God bestowed upon him.

Rabbi Mordechai of Lechovitz

When going before the final judgment,
one is asked:
"Have you conducted your business in
good faith?" (Talmud, *Shabbat* 31a)
What they are really asking is:
In business negotiations, you do your
best to increase your profit.
Have you negotiated in good faith to
strengthen and build your faith
as well?"

Rabbi Menachem Mendel of Kotzk

How can one speak falsehood while
chanting the words:
"And on your great lovingkindness do
we truly and completely rely"?

Rabbi Moshe Leib of Sassov

How easy it is for the poor person to
trust in God, for who else can such a
person trust?
And how difficult it is for a rich person
to trust in God, since one's
possessions cry out, "Trust in us!"

Rabbi Moshe of Kobrin

"God's Greatness cannot be *fathomed*."
(Psalms 145:3)
Meaning: God's Greatness cannot be
determined through scientific
inquiry, but only through faith.[1]

Rabbi Menachem Mendel of Kotzk

"[If a person says,] I have labored and I
have found, believe him." (Talmud,
Megillah 6b)
Meaning: You can find faith once you
have labored in the Torah.

---

1. Play on Hebrew *heker*, 'fathomed', and *hakira*,
'inquiry.'

Rabbi Yaakov Yitzchak of Pshis'cha

"You shall be my treasured possession."
   (Exodus 19:5)
What does "treasured possession" mean?
When people get hold of a remedy to
   cure ills and pains they do not know
   exactly what it is or how it goes
   about healing.
That is how you should be "a treasured
   possession"—with complete and
   utter belief—without trying to be
   overly inquisitive—but rather, with
   a plain and simple faith.

Rabbi Aharon of Starosoli

Faith and security were given hand
   in hand.
The faithful are secure.
And those who are insecure—it is surely
   a sign that they lack faith.

TRUTH

Rabbi Yisrael of Rizhin
_____

All of the world's crowns are destined to
    fall by the wayside except for
    the Crown of Truth—which will
    last forever.

Rabbi Menachem Mendel of Kotzk
_____

Truth must peck at the brain
    like the gnat did to Titus.[1]

_____

1. The Talmud tells us that a gnat pecked at Titus's
brain for seven years (Talmud, *Gittin* 56b)

Rabbi Nachman of Bratzlav

A truthful person can always tell
whether someone is telling the
truth or not.

Rabbi Menachem Mendel of Kotzk

Throughout my life I have never
regretted telling the truth.

Rabbi Menachem Mendel of Kotzk

Everything in this world can be
imitated except for the truth.
Because an artificial, counterfeit truth is
not the truth at all.

Rabbi Nachman of Bratzlav

There is only one truth.
Many truths are but one big lie.

Rabbi Nachman of Bratzlav

When there is no truth, there is neither
faith nor lovingkindness.

Rabbi Pinchas of Koretz

The biggest liars are occupied with
thoughts of sin and heresy, because
truth and faith go hand in hand.

Baal Shem Tov

"Truth springs up from the Earth."
(Psalms 85:12)
If so, then why do not people pull this
treasure out from the Earth?
Because they are too lazy to bend
their backs.

Rabbi Moshe Chaim Ephraim Sadilkov

"Truth springs up from the Earth."
(Psalms 85:12)
Those who want to get nearer to the
truth must crouch down to the dust
and raise it from there.

Rabbi Moshe of Kobrin

People would be better off abstaining
from lying than abstaining from
food and drink.

Rabbi Pinchas of Koretz

I labored twenty-one years to discover
the Truth.
Seven years to recognize what the Truth
is, seven years to drive out
Falsehood, seven years to fill my
inner self with Truth.

Rabbi Simcha Bunam of Pshis'cha

What is the difference between "loving
truth" and "hating falsehood"?
One who hates falsehood hates
the entire world, because
there is no one who is not a
little false.
One who loves truth loves the
entire world, because there is
no one who does not harbor a
little truth.

Rabbi Pinchas of Koretz

Nothing has been as difficult as my
effort to rid my spirit of falsehoods.
It took me twenty-one years to do
and broke my legs and limbs.

Rabbi Yaakov Yitzchak of Pshis'cha

Many people love falsehood
and only a few love truth.
For it is possible to love falsehood truly,
but it is impossible to love
truth falsely.

Rabbi Nachman of Bratslav

It is better even to trust in lies and
nonsense—so that you may believe
in the truth as well— than it is to
deny everything.

Rabbi Menachem Mendel of Rimanov

Even one who is a liar by nature
cannot stand being lied to.

Rabbi Simcha Bunam of Pshis'cha

It is an accepted fact that harlotry is a
sin, and no one would ever say that
it is a commandment.
It is not so with falsehood, which is the
worst sin there is.
Yet there are times when some act as if
it were a commandment.

Rabbi Hersch Leib of Ulik

"Elijah will come . . . only to distance
those who are close, and to bring
close those who are distant."
(Mishnah, *Eduyot* 8:7)
Who are "those who are distant"? The
letters of the Hebrew word for
'Truth', which are distant from
one another.[2]
And who are "those who are close"? The
letters of the Hebrew word for
'Falsehood', which are close to
one another.[3]

Rabbi Simcha Bunam of Autvitzk

No insult is more likely to annoy a liar
as much as being suspected of lying.

Rabbi Nachman of Bratzlav

A person would be better off dead
than to be known as a liar.

---

2. The letters that make up the Hebrew word *emet*,
'truth', are at the very beginning, middle, and end of
the Hebrew alphabet—far apart from one another.

3. The letters that make up the Hebrew word *sheker*,
'falsehood', are contiguous in the Hebrew alphabet.

Rabbi Pinchas of Koretz

It is better that one's soul departs from
the body, than a false word departs
from the mouth.

Rabbi Nachman of Bratzlav

When you see liars, rest assured that
their leader is a liar as well.

Rabbi Nachman of Bratzlav

By way of the vanity of beauty
do we get to the charm of falsehood.

Rabbi Naftali of Ropshitz

Rivka knew that it would be difficult for
Yaakov to tell a lie, because Yaakov
was honest by nature—thus the
verse "Be true to Yaakov."
(Micah 7:20)
That is why she dressed him in the
clothing of Esav.
Because when one dresses like Esav
one assimilates a small measure of
his disposition.

Rabbi Zussya of Anapoli

"Distance yourself from speaking
falsely." (Exodus 23:7)
One distances oneself from God by
speaking falsely—even once,
because "One who speaks falsely
cannot stand before God's eyes."
(Psalms 101:7)

SELF-CENTEREDNESS

Rabbi Menachem Mendel of Kotzk

> The "I"
> is a hidden thief.

Rabbi Dov Ber of Mezritch

> "I stood between God and you."
> (Deuteronomy 5:5)
> Self-centeredness is the screen that
> separates people and God.

SIGHS

Rabbi Menachem Mendel of Kotzk

The entire world is not worth one sigh.

Rabbi Menachem of Bratzlav

A sigh will make you a whole new person, in body and soul.

THE CREATOR
AND THE CREATION

Rabbi Levi Yitzchak of Berditchev

Everyone knows the price of things
     but few know their true value.
Everyone knows that there is a Creator
     but few know God's true value.

Rabbi Dov Ber of Mezritch

"The earth is full of Your creations."
     (Psalms 104:24)
The earth is full of possessions
     [creations] through which one can
     possess godliness.

53

Rabbi Dov Ber of Mezritch

There is even a spark of divinity in
idols, which both gives them life
and eventually destroys them.

Rabbi Yaakov Yosef of Polnoye

Nature itself is the Divine Presence.

Baal Shem Tov

When you look upon the world,
you are looking upon its Creator.

Rabbi Pinchas of Koretz

Matchmaking partakes something of the
creation of the world.

Rabbi Nachman of Bratzlav

Woe is us! The world is full of light and
mysteries both wonderful and
awesome but our tiny little hand
shades our eyes and prevents them
from seeing.

Rabbi Moshe Chaim Ephraim of Sadilkov

The Divine Presence includes each and
every world: plant-life, wildlife,
inanimate, and animate.

Baal Shem Tov

Every speck of dust
overflows with Divine vitality.

Rabbi Simcha Bunam of Pshis'cha

Whoever doubts that each grain of sand
should be nowhere else but exactly
where it is is indeed a heretic who
doubts God's personal providence.

YOUTH AND OLD AGE

Rabbi Nachman of Bratzlav

Do not ever grow old.
Not even as a righteous old person, or a
   charitable one.
Old age is a deplorable trait.
People must always rejuvenate
   themselves.
Beginning, moving forward, going back,
   and starting over again.

Rabbi Tzvi Hirsch of Tomashov

Old age is not always a result of years.
There are those who are born old.
After all, I have seen stale dough baked
   with my own two eyes.

Rabbi Yitzchak Eizik of Komarna

> In my youth I believed that I would
>   ascend to the heavens in a
>   whirlwind like Elijah.
> Now that I have grown old, I say:
> I hope at least I do not plummet down
>   to the bowels of hell.
> Had I not stopped believing as I used to,
>   who knows how low I might be
>   right now . . .

Rabbi Menachem Mendel of Kotzk

> Just as apes imitate humans, so do the
>   elderly imitate themselves,
>   and behave as they did before
>   they aged.

Rabbi Ber of Ostrovtsa

> When an old person dies, all people
>   nod their heads:
> "They were old."
> I don't get it:
> Do the old really deserve the
>   death penalty?

Rabbi Menachem Mendel of Kotzk

"Educate a youth the right way,
And he will not turn from it, even in old
    age." (Proverbs 22:6)
Only if he continues to educate himself
    in his old age.

PERSON TO PERSON

Rabbi Chanoch Henich of Alexander

When people grow tall [in spirit], they
do no harm to their fellows, but
when they grow wide [in ego]—they
butt up against their neighbors.

Rabbi Ze'ev of Strikov

"Walk before me and be innocent."
(Genesis 17:1)
Behaving innocently can only be done
before God.
To behave innocently with other people
is a difficult thing indeed.

Rabbi Menachem Mendel of Kotzk

There are those who keep [observe] the
    pleasant and easy parts of the
    Torah for themselves, and leave
    the difficult parts for others
    [to observe].

Rabbi Simcha Bunam of Pshis'cha

I love those who are abandoned,
    but only if they have abandoned
    themselves and not others.

Rabbi Yaakov Yosef of Polnoye

If one does not recognize one's own
    worth, how can one appreciate the
    worth of another?

Rabbi Yitzchak of Vorki

Sugar, which disappears completely in
    water—still sweetens.
Likewise, people who pay no heed
    to themselves are still able to
    help others.

Baal Shem Tov

The blessing of a friend is of the utmost importance in Heaven—even more than a recommendation from the Angel Michael.

Rabbi Yerachmiel Yisrael Yitzchak Danziger

To be worthy of offering advice to another one need not be an expert. It is sufficient to be a trusted friend.

Rabbi Meir of Premishlan

People were given two eyes so that they could see their friends' merits with one eye, and their own defects with the other.

Rabbi Avraham of Sochatchov

If the persecuted knew what a favor their persecutors were doing them, they would turn around and give chase to kiss the hems of their gowns.

Baal Shem Tov

Just as people who look into a mirror
see their own blemishes, so those
who see faults in others know that
they share some of the same fault.

Rabbi Mendel of Zlotchov

Those who do not commiserate with the
sorrows of their friends can be sure
that their ancestors were not
present at Mount Sinai.

Rabbi Yitzchak Zelig of Sokolov

To suffer torments is easier than to
justify them.
To share in the sorrows of your friend is
easier than to justify them.

Rabbi Menachem Mendel of Kotzk

Just as we accept that our neighbor's
face does not resemble ours, so
must we accept that our neighbor's
views do not resemble ours.

Rabbi Nachman of Bratzlav

Those who infringe on the livelihood
of others, it is as if they seduced
their spouse.

Rabbi Nachman of Bratslav

Better to violate a biblical command,
than to embarrass another
human being.

Rabbi Yitzchak Meir of Ger

A person finding a worn-out penny on
the ground, would immediately
bend over to pick it up.
Yet in relating to other humans,
one would raise oneself to the
Heavens, yet refuse to lower oneself
even the tiniest drop.

Baal Shem Tov

"Who is wise? One who learns from
everyone." (Mishnah, *Avot* 4:1)
Those who can see their own faults in
the flaws of others.

Rabbi Aharon of Karlin

"You shall not make for yourself a
   sculptured image."[1] (Exodus 20:4)
Do not make of yourself one who rejects
   other people's ideas out of hand.

Baal Shem Tov

People live for seventy years.
Could they not do something just once
   to make someone else's life better?

Rabbi Baruch of Medzibuz

People are very careful not to swallow
   an insect, but they are not careful
   about devouring a person.

Rabbi Menachem Mendel of Kotzk

"And you shall be a holy people unto
   Me." (Exodus 22:30)
Let your holiness be humane,
   reasonable, and acceptable to others.

---

1. Play on Hebrew *pesel*, 'sculptured image', and
posel, 'reject.'

Rabbi Moshe of Kobrin

My father used to say to me
    that in addition to the four chapters
    of the code of behavior, the
    Shulkhan Arukh, there is a need for
    a fifth chapter that teaches one how
    to behave with others.
I think that there should be a sixth
    chapter as well:
How to behave with those who do not
    merit good treatment.

Rabbi Yitzchak Eizik of Ziditzov

The golden rule: give and take.
That is the way the world was created.
So that everyone should influence
    others and be influenced in kind.
Anyone who does not embody both of
    these qualities is nothing but a
    fruitless tree.

Rabbi Chaim Halberstam of Tzanz

I am so confused!
If one says "I am poor," few believe him.
Yet if one says: "I am a criminal and a
    thief," everyone believes him!

"The Holy Jew" of Pshis'cha

There is a spark of holiness even
in heresy.
One who sees others stumble and fall
must strive to help them, and
not say:
"They are on the brink of falling—that is
the will of God."

Rabbi Menachem Mendel of Kotzk

"When the people saw it they moved
back and stood at a distance."
(Exodus 20:15)
People can see, people can be moved
and astonished, and, nevertheless,
still keep their distance.

Baal Shem Tov

"Do not be a talebearer *among* your
people." (Leviticus 19:16)
Do not spread gossip *about* your
people."[2]

---

2. Play on Hebrew preposition *b*, which can mean
both "among" and "about."

Rabbi Menachem Mendel of Kotzk

"You shall appoint yourself judges and
officials." (Deuteronomy 16:18)
"You shall appoint yourself" means "for
you, yourself."
Scrutinize your own deeds and pass
judgment on yourself, before you
judge others.

Rabbi Yaakov Yosef of Polnoye

"Faithful are the wounds of a friend."
(Proverbs 27:6)
Just as a healing doctor is the first to
discover a wound, so is one who
finds fault with friends the first to
admonish them.

Rabbi Avraham Yaakov of Sadigora

"There is nothing which does not have
its place." (Mishnah, *Avot* 4:3)
If that is so, then everyone has a place
as well.
So why does it often seem that our
space is so limited?
Because everyone is scrambling to take
everyone else's spot.

Baal Shem Tov

"People see all afflictions save their
    own." (Mishnah, *Negaim* 2:5)
Meaning: All of the afflictions that
    people see around them are really
    just a product of their own flaws—
    because those who reject others
    are really just rejecting their
    own shortcomings.

The Seer of Lublin

Two pious people in one town are
    too many.
One pious person in a town is
    not enough.
It is best to have one-and-a-half
    pious people.
How so? Everyone should see oneself as
    half of a pious person, and see one's
    neighbor as a complete pious person.
Then each will defer to the other.

THE INNER SELF

Rabbi Chanoch Henich of Alexander

Behold, I am a creature of this world.
I was created with two eyes and
    two arms.
All of my limbs and organs are healthy.
Yet I have no idea for what purpose I
    was created, or what I am supposed
    to fix in this world.

Rabbi Mordechai of Lechovitz

If your life is not going according to
    your will, mold your will according
    to your life.

Rabbi Chaim Halberstam of Tzanz

Those who consider themselves
    nobodies lack for nothing
    because nothing lacks for nothing.

Rabbi Nachman of Bratslav

Someone who does not reserve
    one hour every day for oneself,
    is not human.

The Seer of Lublin

Is it really such a big deal to be a
    great person?
Anyone, no matter what their standing,
    can mix heaven and earth!
But to be a *good* person . . . that is a great
    deed indeed!

Rabbi Shlomo of Radomsk

There is no creature as crooked as
    human beings.
Humans are born with two legs with
    which to walk, yet they use their
    elbows to get ahead.

Rabbi Menachem Mendel of Kotzk

If I am who I am because I am who I
    am, and you are who you are
    because you are who you are,
    then I am who I am and you are
    who you are.
But if I am who I am because you are
    who you are and you are who you
    are because I am who I am
    then I am not I nor are you, you.

Rabbi Moshe of Karlin

Only after one has been set free
    can one feel the bitterness
    of slavery.

Rabbi Izel Charif

Beasts fill up their bellies.
Humans must fill up their heads.

Rabbi Pinchas of Koretz

There are creatures who spend all of
    their time eating, but their time in
    this world is short.

Rabbi Baruch of Medzibuz

Everyone was created to right
    something in this world.
Either they owe it to the world
    or the world owes it to them.

Rabbi Nachman of Bratslav

If we are not better tomorrow than we
    are today, why have a tomorrow?

Rabbi Uri of Strelisk

None of us serves our generation alone.
For example, David continues to inspire
    the downcast with his fiery passion,
    generation after generation.
And Samson's heroics continue to give
    courage to the meek 'til this day.

Rabbi Menachem Mendel of Kotzk

I would hope that even if the sky were
    to fall and the earth to crumble,
    that humans would hold fast to
    their place and not budge from it.

The Maggid of Trisk

Most people are like a metal oven:
burning one minute like a flame,
but a short time later—as cold as ice.

Rabbi Simcha Bunam of Pshis'cha

Millions of people are born like mice,
live like mice and die like mice.
Make sure you are not one of them.

Rabbi Chanoch Henich of Alexander

There is clear evidence that no one is in
need of a servant.
Case in point: you were born
without one.

Rabbi Menachem Mendel of Kotzk

One is created alone and must always
remain in one's aloneness.

Rabbi Tzvi Elimelech of Dinov

One who is never ashamed of oneself,
has no shame whatsoever.

Rabbi Noah of Lechovitz

The sages say:
Each person is like "a world
    in miniature."
This means that if people are a "world"
    in their own eyes, then they can be
    considered as "miniature."
And if they are "miniature" in their own
    eyes, then they can be considered to
    be a whole "world."

Rabbi Dov Ber of Mezritch

The essence of human beings is in their
    image—the human character that is
    reflected in it.

Rabbi Avraham Yehoshua Heschel of Apta

A person needs to be like a vessel that
    accepts all that its owner pours into
    it—whether it be wine, or vinegar.

Rabbi Nachman of Bratslav

It takes hard work to impersonate a
    great sage.

Rabbi Shalom Rokeach of Belz

Each person can be compared to an
impure vessel.
As long as the vessel is whole, there is
no problem.
It can be washed, cleaned, and returned
to its purity.

Rabbi Menachem Mendel of Kotzk

I can tell you what should not be done—
but as for what should be done . . .
that is something we all must
figure out for ourselves.

Rabbi Shneur Zalman of Liadi

The ground calls out to humankind:
Why do you trample all over me?
Are you really any better than I?

Rabbi Yitzchak of Vorki

It is true that Yom Kippur atones for
one's sins.
But to become pure, that one must
achieve oneself.

Rabbi Menachem Mendel of Vitebsk

I have no idea how I am any better than
a worm.
I do not know if I am even as good
as one.
Case in point:
The worm goes about its way without
destroying a thing.

Rabbi Menachem Mendel of Kotzk

If God were to show you your true
colors, you would not be able to
continue living for a single hour.

Rabbi Zussya of Anapoli

Oh ground below me,
you are greater than I.
Though I stomp on you with my feet,
soon enough, I will be lying beneath
you, defeated.

Baal Shem Tov

Wherever our will directs us—
there will we find our place.

Rabbi Tsadok HaKohen of Lublin

> The place where people flee in their
>   hour of trouble—that is where their
>   roots lie.

Rabbi Yisrael of Rizhin

> Humans should act like clocks.
> When a house goes up in flames the
>   clock on the wall does not get
>   worked up about it, it just keeps
>   on doing what it was doing
>   without deviating, so long as it does
>   not catch fire itself.

Rabbi Menachem Mendel of Kotzk

> I ask only three things of you:
> Do not be a flatterer by nature.
> Do not flatter or fawn upon
>   your neighbor.
> And do not think only of yourself.

Rabbi Menachem Mendel of Kotzk

> Those who can curse themselves, are
>   capable of cursing the entire world.

Rabbi Simcha Bunam of Pshis'cha

Every person should have two pockets.
In one should be a piece of paper on
    which is written: "I am but dust
    and ashes."
In the other: "For my sake was the
    world created."

Rabbi Aharon of Karlin

If we do not arrive at a new insight
    every day, it is a sign that we also
    have acquired nothing of others'
    old insights.

Rabbi Pinchas of Koretz

I am forever afraid that I will never be
    wiser than I am pious.

Rabbi Eliyahu of Viskut

People are always scrutinizing their
    deeds to find out why they have
    been chosen to suffer so.
I have yet to see someone who
    contemplates why they merited
    such wealth and happiness.

Rabbi Menachem Mendel of Kotzk

One's freedom is more important even
than studying God's ways.
Therefore, Jews must immerse
themselves in stories of their
departure from bondage and the
Exodus from Egypt even more than
they should immerse themselves in
a difficult passage from the Talmud.

Rabbi Simcha Bunam of Pshis'cha

Jews in the midst of fasting are
convinced that they will become
angels one day.
But they prove time and again that once
the fast is over, they eat like mere
mortals—at times they munch more
greedily than a horse!

Rabbi Ze'ev of Strikov

It takes a person a year or two to learn a
foreign language.
But it is doubtful that seventy years are
enough to understand one's own
internal language.

Rabbi Menachem Mendel of Kotzk

To get away with the minimum
        standard of the law?
Never!
It is all or nothing!

Rabbi Yitzchak Meir of Ger

There are only two who truly know you:
God and your spouse.

Rabbi Tsadok HaKohen of Lublin

Just as it is difficult for the wicked to
        appreciate the needs of their
        friends, likewise is it difficult for the
        good to appreciate their own needs.

Rabbi Shmuel of Sokhotchov

"Go forth. . . . " (Genesis 12:1)
Go unto yourself, be what you
        truly are.[1]

---

1. Play on Hebrew *Lech lecha*, meaning 'Go forth',
or 'Go to yourself.'

Rabbi Pinchas of Koretz

Every person possesses one valuable
trait that cannot be found in
any other.

Rabbi Menachem Mendel of Kotzk

I do not fear the suffering of illness,
but rather, the pampering
that follows.

Rabbi Menachem Mendel of Kotzk

"Beware of going up the mountain or
touching its flanks." (Exodus 19:12)
You have started up the mountain.
Conquer it all!

Rabbi Menachem Mendel of Kotzk

"Send forth men [to scout the land of
Canaan. . . .]" (Numbers 13:2)
Send forth that which is human from
within you.[2]

---

2. Play on Hebrew *anashim*, "men", and *enoshi*,
"human."

Rabbi Chanoch Henich of Alexander

"The Heavens belong to God!
But the earth God gave to humankind."
    (Psalms 115:16)
The Heavens are heavenly in any event.
God gave the earth to humans so that
    they could make that which is
    worldly, heavenly.

Rabbi Zelig of Sharansk

Why did the Rabbi cry when he said:
"Are there those among us who can
    acquire their world in a single
    hour?" (Talmud, *Avodah Zarah* 6b)
Because something that can be acquired
    in a single hour can be lost in half
    an hour.

Rabbi Menachem Mendel of Kotzk

"And the mountain went up in flames
    to the heart of the Heavens."
    (Deuteronomy 4:11)
When does a mountain go up in flames?
When the heart becomes Heavenly.

Rabbi Menachem Mendel of Kotzk

"Listen, Oh Heavens. . . . "
(Deuteronomy 32:1)
Listen in a Heavenly manner.

Rabbi Menachem Mendel of Kotzk

"[If someone says to you,] I struggled
but still did not discover, do not
believe him." (Talmud, *Megillah* 6b)
Because the struggle in and of itself is a
great discovery, a great find indeed.

Rabbi Zussya of Anapoli

If they ask me in Heaven, "Why were
you not Moses?" I will know how
to answer.
But if they ask me, "Why were you not
Zussya?" I will have no reply.

Rabbi Menachem Mendel of Kotzk

"You shall not steal." (Exodus 20:13)
You shall not steal your self.
Meaning: Do not deceive yourself.

Rabbi Menachem Mendel of Kotzk

The size of a person's soul
    can be measured by the stature of
    the person who surrounds it.
Much like a precious stone:
    the more valuable the gem, the
    larger the setting.

BODY AND SOUL

The Baal Shem Tov

Even a holy body
is just flesh.

Rabbi Nachman of Bratslav

Heal your body
before you heal your soul.

Rabbi Elimelech of Lizhensk

There is no such thing as materialism
that does not possess a spark of
the spiritual.

Baal Shem Tov

In the materialistic world,
> where there is awe, there is no
> happiness and where there is
> happiness, there is no awe.

In the spiritual world,
> where there is awe, there is love and
> happiness as well.

Rabbi Menachem Mendel of Kotzk

There are those who want to travel to
> Israel in order to avoid the tortures
> of "the rolling of the dead."[1]

It really makes me wonder.

They must really love their bodies so
> much that they dread suffering
> even after death.

Rabbi Menachem Mendel of Kotzk

It is easier for the body to endure
> fasting and self-mortification
> than to bear the yoke of Heaven.

---

1. There is a religious belief that those buried outside of Israel will roll there at the time of the resurrection of the dead.

Rabbi Elimelech of Lizhensk

A person's true dwelling place is in the
Heavenly World above.

Baal Shem Tov

"To be for you your God."
(Leviticus 11:45)
Even the material acts that you
perform "for you" should be
performed for the sake of God.

Rabbi Yaakov of Polnoye

When the body feels pleasure—the soul
aches, and when the soul feels
pleasure—the body aches.

Rabbi Yaakov of Polnoye

Too much oil puts out the lamp.

Rabbi Simcha Bunam of Pshis'cha

When I take out a soul to wash and
clean it, it loses a lot of blood.

Rabbi Chaim of Chenaz

The soul is not concerned with
mundane matters such as food
and drink.
Nevertheless, when denied food and
drink, it escapes from the body and
flies away.

Rabbi Dov Ber of Mezritch

"And the earth became corrupt before
God." (Genesis 6:11)
The sin of Noah's generation was
that they put the earth before God.
They made earthiness primary, and
God secondary.

Rabbi Shmelke of Nikolsburg

"I will establish my dwelling place
among you, and My soul will not
treat you with scorn."
(Leviticus 26:11)
So that the soul will not scorn the body
[the dwelling place of the soul].

Baal Shem Tov

The soul is like a candle.
At times the candle is lit and at times it
    is out.
Such is the soul—at times lit and at
    other times out.

Rabbi Shmuel Horovitz

Since every person's soul is in part
    Divine, we must pity the Godly
    spark that is imprisoned inside of
    an evil person, and offer it our love.

HEAVEN AND HELL

Rabbi Aryeh Leib, the Grandfather of Shpoli

If we only read about sin in books
      and Hell were an actual place in
      this world, then no one would be
      caught sinning.
But what can you do?
Sin does exist in this world, and Hell we
      read about only in books.

Rabbi Simcha Bunam of Pshis'cha

Look how foolish humans are!
The path to Heaven is open, and no
      one enters.
And yet the gates to Hell they rush to
      break down.

Rabbi Zussya of Anapoli

"The impudent ['strong-headed'] are
   sent to Hell." (Mishnah, *Avot* 5:20)
Those of strong spirit, who do not
   frighten easily, can go even to the
   nethermost depths of Hell and still
   have nothing to fear.

EXILE AND REDEMPTION

Rabbi Yehuda Aryeh Leib of Ger

> You can be in exile in your own house
> when you realize that you are not
> really at home.

Rabbi Aryeh Leib, the Grandfather of Shpoli

> Ruler of the Universe:
> You have exiled your children so that
> they would mend their ways,
> but I swear this will not do them
> any good.
> Just try sending Your righteous Messiah
> and see how they run after him.

Rabbi David of Sochatchov

> All of the comforts of exile
>   are nothing but a diversion
>   to make us forget that we are
>   indeed exiled.

Rabbi Nachman of Bratslav

> The source of exile
>   is lack of faith.

Baal Shem Tov

> What does Exile really mean?
> That wisdom has been exiled.

Rabbi Yaakov Yosef of Polnoye

> There are three types of exiles:
> The exile of the Children of Israel
>   among the peoples of the world;
> The exile of the Children of the Book
>   among the ignorant;
> And the exile of the faithful and
>   righteous among the treacherous.

Rabbi Yaakov Yosef of Polnoye

There are three types of exiles:
The exile of the Divine Presence;
The exile of the spirit;
And the exile of the body.

Rabbi Mordechai of Ger

For the redemption to arrive, two things
must happen:
The Israelite people must be taken out
of exile.
And the exile must be taken out of the
Israelite people.
The latter is more difficult than
the former.

Rabbi Shlomo of Karlin

" . . . who freed you from the travails of
Egypt." (Exodus 6:7)
The root of the biblical Hebrew for
'travails' is the same as that of
'forbearance.'
Because the Israelites' prolonged exile
in Egypt prepared them to bear
whatever may come.

Rabbi Shalom Rokeach of Belz

There are three exiles:
Exile among the gentiles;
Exile among other Jews;
And exile from one's own self.

Rabbi Simcha Bunam of Pshis'cha

Ruler of the Universe:
Redeem the Jews while they are
    still Jews.
Otherwise, you may one day have to
    redeem them as gentiles.

Rabbi Moshe of Pshevorsk

Do not despair of the redemption,
    because the Divine Presence is in
    the exile as well.
So for God's own sake you too will
    be redeemed.

Rabbi Yisrael of Kozhnitz

Ruler of the Universe, I pray of You,
    redeem the People of Israel.
And if that is not Your will, then redeem
    the gentiles.

Rabbi Pinchas of Koretz

> Are you so sure that the wicked are
>> delaying the redemption?
> Heaven forbid! The "good Jews" are the
>> ones delaying it.
> A nail hanging on a wall will not disturb
>> a thing.
> But a needle left in a shirt will
>> prick you!

Rabbi Yechiel Michal of Zlotchov

> "Those whom God loves, He rebukes."
>> (Proverbs 3:12)
> One who truly loves God must justify
>> why God does not redeem
>> His children.

Rabbi Yisrael of Kozhnitz

> "Raise the glory of Israel Your people"
>> (from the prayer "Our Father
>> Our King")
> Lift up and raise the glory of Israel now;
>> do not wait for the Redemption.

WORRY

Rabbi Mordechai of Lechovitz

All worrying is forbidden,
    except to worry that one is worried.

Rabbi Yechiel Michal of Zlotchov

I learned this wisdom from
    my ancestors:
There are two things it is forbidden to
    worry about:
That which it is possible to fix, And that
    which it is impossible to fix.
What is possible to fix—fix it, and
    why worry?
What is impossible to fix—how will
    worrying help?

Rabbi Yitzchak Eizik of Komarna

Everyone needs a little worrying
or suffering.
A ship without any cargo will list
and is even liable to capsize.

Rabbi Ze'ev Wolf of Zhitomir

Rather than worrying about what to do
tomorrow, you are better off fixing
what you did yesterday.

Rabbi Yitzchak of Vorka

"You shall no longer give the people
straw." (Exodus 5:7)
Would it not have been better for the
Egyptians to continue giving the
slaves straw so that they would
increase the number of bricks they
could make?
From this we learn that burdening one's
mind and heart is more difficult on
the body than hard labor.

Rabbi Moshe of Kobrin

> If I knew for sure that I said "Amen"
> properly even once, then I would
> never worry again.

Speech and Silence

Rabbi Menachem Mendel of Vorki

Silence without substance is
also worthy.
But speech without substance is but
idle blather.

Rabbi Avraham of Trisk

You do not need to speak to yourself,
just thinking to yourself is enough.
So why speak at all? For the benefit
of others?
Perhaps they are not in need of this
great service either.

Rabbi Dov Ber of Mezritch

Speech is the dress of thought.
When one speaks, one's thoughts
are revealed.

Rabbi Yitzchak Meir of Ger

What is the oral law?
The law handed down by those
who were Rulers over their
own mouths.[1]

Baal Shem Tov

"Make an opening for light for the ark."
(Genesis 6:16)
The biblical Hebrew word for 'ark' also
means 'word.'
If we read the biblical text in this way
we learn that when people speak,
their thoughts should enlighten
their speech.

Rabbi Menachem Mendel of Kotzk

Silence is the sweetest of sounds.

---

1. Play on Hebrew *b'al peh,* meaning both 'oral'
and 'ruler over their mouth.'

"The Holy Jew" of Pshis'cha

There is no organ more cumbersome
    than the tongue.
It is always in need of someone else to
    hear its words.
Yet there is nothing so adroit as silence,
    which has no need of any
    outside support.

Rabbi Mendel of Vorki

Learn to be silent—so that you may learn
    to speak.

Baal Shem Tov

The sounds of silence are more elevated
    than the sounds of speech.

Rabbi Nachman of Bratslav

As children we learn to speak.
As elders we learn silence.
And this is the great flaw we have —
    to learn to speak before we learn to
    be quiet.

Rabbi Dov Ber of Mezritch

Haste is a positive and precious trait
for all one's limbs, except the mouth
and the tongue.

Rabbi Nachman of Bratslav

One can scream
with a still, small voice.

Rabbi Menachem Mendel of Kotzk

When one has something to scream
about, and wants to scream,
but cannot scream,
that is the loudest scream of all!

Rabbi Yitzchak of Vorki

Solitude is good for the soul, indeed, it
is good for everything.
But the key to solitude is to be alone
while still in the company of others.
Those who are completely alone and
silent cannot claim that they have
conquered their appetite for speech.

Rabbi Chaim Meir Yehiel of Moglenitza

Not only are great eaters and drinkers
    gluttons and drunks
    but idle chatterers as well:
    the former with what they put in
    their mouths and the latter with
    what they let out.

Rabbi Mendel of Vorki

A shout which comes from the heart—
    even one that does not cross the
    lips—still splits the skies and rips
    through the heavens.

Rabbi Avraham Yaakov of Sadigora

No one ever tires of silence.

Rabbi Izel of Slonim

"Silence is a fence for wisdom."
    (Mishnah, *Avot* 3:17)
Silence is indeed a fence for wisdom,
    but it is not the whole matter.
No one has become wise through
    silence alone.

Rabbi Menachem Mendel of Vorki

A horse is very sparing of words;
 in fact he never speaks at all.
Yet he is not considered righteous.
He is just a horse.
A person who has the virtue of limiting
 idle speech is one who is silent even
 in the few words that he utters.

Rabbi Ze'ev of Strikov

A quiet person is not one who holds his
 tongue when he has nothing to say.
That person simply shows that he is
 not a fool.
One who holds his tongue is quiet
 despite the fact that he has
 something to say.

LAW AND JUSTICE

Rabbi Dov Ber of Mezritch

In every judgment there is mercy.

Rabbi Nachman of Bratslav

Compromise is the sign of a trial
where justice has been served.

Rabbi Simcha Bunam of Pshis'cha

"Do not render an unjust decision."
(Leviticus 19:15)
Do not grant injustice legitimacy by way
of a trial.

Rabbi Yerachmiel Yisrael Danziger

"You shall not covet." (Exodus 20:14)
To measure the degree of this
  infraction, you need a scale of gold.

The Holy Jew

"Justice, justice shall you pursue."
  (Deuteronomy 16:20)
Even your pursuit of justice must be
  with justice and not with fraud.

Rabbi David of Luba

"Before whom is the soul to give
  judgment and account?" (Mishnah,
  Avot 3:1)
Is not the expression backwards? Does
  not the account precede the
  judgment?
The Heavenly Court always asks the
  soul being judged:
What judgment would *you* think proper
  for someone who commits such and
  such a sin?
After the soul answers, it is told, "You
  committed such a sin," and an
  accounting is made.

CRYING AND TEARS

Rabbi Pinchas of Koretz

All the world's spheres and souls help
    us weep and shed our tears.
When tears fall from our eyes, the mind
    is cleared because releasing tears
    cleanses the brain.

Rabbi Simcha Bunam of Pshis'cha

I have learned: "The gates of tears shall
    not be locked."
Then why have gates at all?
For those fools who cry
      but have no idea what they are
      crying about.

Rabbi Nachman of Bratslav

> Man is like an onion.
> When you peel away the layers,
>   all that is left is tears.

Rabbi Yechiel Danziger

> Tears may also be bribes.

Rabbi Pinchas of Koretz

> When a child is small, he cries
>   without inhibition.
> But when he reaches the stage of
>   consciousness, he loses the ability
>   to cry.

Rabbi Nachum of Chernobyl

> What Leah achieved by crying
> Rachel achieved by smiling.

LEADERSHIP AND AUTHORITY

The Holy Jew

> A leader of the masses is like a
>   launderer who bleaches wool in
>   the sun:
> The wool whitens, but the launderer
>   himself comes out black.

Rabbi Yitzchak Meir of Ger

> For a great generation, weak leaders
>   are sufficient.
> A weak generation requires
>   great leaders, just as a dangerously
>   sick person requires a great expert
>   who will cure him of his illness.

115

Rabbi Izel Charif

A rabbi who cannot preach
    is like a coachman without a whip.
And a preacher who cannot act as rabbi,
    is like a whip without a coachman.

Rabbi Mendele of Kuzov

When I exhort and admonish
    my congregation it is not directed
    towards anyone specifically.
Yet, if some think that I am directing
    my words towards them,
    then indeed, I am.

Rabbi Nachman of Bratslav

There are leaders who cannot even
    lead themselves, much less others.
Yet they presume to have the authority
    to lead the entire world.

Rabbi Mordechai Yosef Leiner of Ishbitz

There are very few among those who
    rule others who rule themselves.

Rabbi Uri of Strelisk

> The great King David himself
> > humbly wrote:
> "I was a brute, without knowledge. . . . "
> > (Psalms 73:22)
> And here am *I*, a leader of Israel,
> > offering advice right and left!

Baal Shem Tov

> "Happy are the people who know how
> > to cry out." (Psalms 89:16)
> It is great when a whole nation
> > recognizes the war cry, and can
> > defend itself against its enemies
> > without having to depend entirely
> > on its leaders.

Rabbi Pinchas of Koretz

> When you arrive at a city and do not
> > know the nature of its people,
> > pay attention to its public servants.
> If they are righteous and wise,
> > so will be the people of the city.
> And if these are not—neither are those.

Rabbi Yechezkel of Kozmir

> Public affairs tended to publicly
>   are greater than Heavenly affairs
>   tended to privately.

Rabbi Asher of Stolin

> One who is exalted and achieves
>   authority nevertheless is in need
>   of followers.
> For what good is a head without legs?

Rabbi Nachman of Bratslav

> One can learn about the leadership of a
>   country by observing the words of
>   its clowns.

The Seer of Lublin

> "Let them judge the people at all
>   times. . . . " (Exodus 18:22)
> God's will shall be judged and
>   determined according to the times.

Rabbi Tzvi Elimelech of Dinov

The amount of a people's guilders
is determined by its guides.

Rabbi Aryeh Leib of Stanislav

Any rabbi who cannot swallow needles
has no business being in
the rabbinate.

SATISFACTION AND SIMPLICITY

Rabbi Yechiel Michal of Zlotchov

> I never needed anything until I already
> had it.
> Because when I did not have it
> I was sure I did not need it.

Rabbi Zussya of Anapoli

> If you say you have no money . . . then
> you speak the truth.
> If you say you need some money . . .
> then you are lying.
> I am never in need of money.

Rabbi Pinchas of Koretz

I accustomed myself not to want
that which I do not want.

INNER THOUGHTS

Rabbi Nachman of Bratslav

> The mind changes directions like the
> flight of a bird, and it takes a great
> deal of strength and wisdom to
> hunt that bird down.

Rabbi Shmuel of Lubavitch

> To have unholy thoughts during prayer
> is both understandable and
> even rational.
> But to have holy thoughts during
> business dealings is not?
> Very surprising!

Rabbi Yitzchak Meir of Ger

> Those who go over past mistakes again
> and again dwell upon evil.
> It is not their thoughts that are tangled
> up, it is they themselves who are
> tangled up in that evil.

Rabbi Meir of Premishlan

> One can tell the nature of a person by
> one's dreams.
> For a person dreams what is in
> the heart, each one with his
> own dreams.
> Father Jacob dreamed of a ladder
> "with its top in the Heavens,
> . . . and Adonai stood beside him."
> (Genesis 28:12–13)
> Pharaoh, on the other hand, dreamed of
> seven beautiful cows.

Rabbi Nachman of Bratslav

> Thoughts are like the pendulum of a
> clock:
> Their movements never cease.

The Seer of Lublin

One who possesses holy thoughts
has senseless ones as well.

Baal Shem Tov

Wherever you find a people's souls you
will find the rest of them as well.

Rabbi Menachem Mendel of Kotzk

Not everything that one thinks, is fit
to say.
Not everything that one says, is fit
to write.
Not everything that one writes, is fit
to publish.

Rabbi Nachman of Bratslav

Tradition says: "When in doubt, it
is preferable not to act."
There are times where this applies
to thought as well as deed,
because even thinking is a type
of deed.

Rabbi Shneur Zalman of Liadi

Contemplating is better than marveling.

Rabbi Menachem Mendel of Kotzk

"How lovely are your feet in sandals. . . . "
    (Song of Songs 7:2)
The heartbeat, and all of the heart's
    emotions are even more beautiful
    when they are kept under lock
    and key. [1]

---

1. Play on Hebrew root *p'm*, source of Hebrew words *p'amayikh*, "your feet", and *p'ima*, "heartbeat." Also, play on the Hebrew root *n'l*, source of *na'alayim*, "sandals", and *n'ulot*, "locked."

FRIENDSHIP AND LONELINESS

Rabbi Yitzchak of Vorki

Being alone has a special value,
 but only when one is among others.

Rabbi Mordechai of Lechovitz

Friendship is like stone.
A stone has no value,
 but by rubbing one stone against
 another, sparks of fire emerge.

Pangs of Messiah

If the Messiah wants to come quietly
    and politely, then we shall wait
    for him.
If he wants to come in fits and throes,
    then let him wait and bide his time.

Rabbi Simcha Bunam of Pshis'cha

Prior to the coming of the Messiah,
    there must be wise people
    without wisdom, pious without
    piety, righteous without
    righteousness and moral people full
    of moral defects.

Rabbi Menachem Mendel of Kossov

> Why has the Messiah not come either
>   yesterday or today?
> Because we are today just as we
>   were yesterday.

Rabbi Nachum of Trisk

> We are commanded to expect the
>   Messiah at any time in order not to
>   believe that he has already come.

Rabbi Mordechai of Lechovitz

> If we believed with a perfect faith in the
>   coming of the Messiah, then we
>   would not wait to read *Lamentations*
>   just once a year on Tisha b'Av.

Rabbi Yisrael of Rizhin

> ". . . Even at evening time will there be
>   light." (Zechariah 14:7)
> God will not cause the Messiah's light to
>   shine until the dusk of twilight.

Rabbi Gedalyahu of Lunitz

Were there no Jews who needed to be
    redeemed, there would be no need
    for a Messiah.

Rabbi Menachem Mendel of Lubavitch

Once the Messiah comes,
    all that is natural
    will seem supernatural.

Rabbi Moshe Teitelbaum

Here I stand, the lowest of the low,
    but a lover of truth nonetheless.
Had I known that the Messiah
    would not have come by the time
    my hair turned gray I would not
    have been able to bear it.
But You, Ruler of the World, still keep
    me waiting, day after day.
What is the big deal in tricking an old
    fool like me?
I beg of you: Let him come! Let him
    come right now!
Not for my sake, for Yours!
So that everyone will sanctify Your
    Holy Name.

LIFE AND DEATH

Rabbi Nachman of Bratslav

One must constantly renew oneself.

Rabbi Simcha Bunam of Pshis'cha

I have been teaching myself how to die
every day of my life.

Rabbi Menachem Mendel of Kotzk

Death is nothing but a move
from one house to another.
If we are wise, we strive to make the
latter the more beautiful home.

Rabbi Menachem Mendel of Kotzk

I have the power to resurrect the dead.
But I would rather resurrect the living.

Rabbi Yitzchak of Vorka

People must first mortify themselves
    in order to truly know how to live.
Once they do that, they will realize
    that they must choose life,
    not death.

Rabbi Moshe HaKohen of Razvadov

I do not fear death.
Indeed, it is what I was born to do.
But I am afraid that I might die like
    an animal.
That is not at all what I was born to do.

Rabbi Nachman of Bratslav

The Angel of Death finds it hard to kill
    all by himself.
That is why they gave him doctors to
    help him.

Rabbi Yehoshua Rokeach of Belz

One must strive to live as a good Jew.
Even Balaam the wicked wanted to die a
     Jew, saying, "May I die the death of
     the upright."
Meaning, he wanted to live as a
     heathen, but die as a Jew.

Rabbi Yitzchak of Vorka

"I shall not die, but live. . . . " (Psalms
     118:17)
Be sure not to be one of the living dead.

Baal Shem Tov

Death is nothing but the passage from
     one corner of the universe
     to another.

WISDOM AND COMMON SENSE

Rabbi Nachman of Bratslav

The greatest bit of cleverness:
   never try to be clever.

Rabbi Naftali of Ropshitz

Humans need a great deal of wisdom
   to be simple.

Rabbi Nachman of Bratslav

You can find some wisdom
   even in debauchery and foolishness.

Rabbi David of Lelov

> Who really knows?
> —Those who know that they do
>   not know.

Rabbi Nachman of Bratslav

> There are those who eat in order to
>   study, and there are those who
>   study to know how to eat.

Rabbi Chanoch Henich HaKohen of Alexander

> "We beseech from You, grant us
>   knowledge and understanding."
>   (from the Amidah prayer)
> We beseech, that we may know
>   that our knowledge and
>   understanding are *from You.*

Rabbi Yehoshua of Ostrovtsa

> One who straightens a ladder, only
>   bends it.
> One who bends a bow, only
>   straightens it.

Baal Shem Tov

Whoever grasps the tip of something
has a grasp on the entire object.

Rabbi Aharon of Karlin

"Every person who is wise of heart. . . ."
(Exodus 36:1)
Wisdom without heart is vain
and empty.

Rabbi Menachem Mendel of Kotzk

"As wisdom grows, torment grows."
(Ecclesiastes 1:18)
And what of this?
Perhaps it is worthwhile to increase
one's torment provided that one
increases one's wisdom as well.

Rabbi Gershon Hanokh of Radzin

I have high regard for the speech of
the wise.
But even more for the silence of
the fool.

Rabbi Moshe Chaim Ephraim Sadilkov

"Who is wise? One who learns from
everyone." (Mishnah, *Avot* 4:1)
Even from the Evil Impulse.

Rabbi Simcha Bunam of Pshis'cha

A fool says what he knows.
A wise person knows what he says.

Rabbi Shalom Dov Ber of Lubavitch

There are two levels of wisdom
and two levels of foolishness:
There are those who are born wise, and
those who acquire wisdom.
Likewise, there are those who are
born fools, and those who
become foolish.

Rabbi Simcha Bunam of Pshis'cha

Every positive command in the Torah
can be summed up thus:
Act wisely.
And every negative command in the
Torah can be summed up thus:
Don't be a fool.

Rabbi Izel Charif

> I have seen a wise person get tripped up
> by foolishness, but I have yet to see
> a fool get tripped by wisdom.

Rabbi Levi Yitzchak of Berditchev

> There is light that is blinding
> and light that is dazzling
> and light that shines only faintly.
> Not so darkness.
> It always darkens in the same measure.
> There are wise people who are brilliant
> and there are those who take a long
> while to discover very little.
> Not so fools.
> They are always just plain foolish.

Rabbi Menachem Mendel of Kotzk

> What is a righteous fool?
> It is one who is fated to be a fool by
> the Heavens who, in his foolishness,
> does many things beyond the strict
> interpretation of the law
> to fulfill the Heavenly decree,
> and, in so doing, adds to his folly.

Rabbi Ze'ev Wolf of Strikov

Why does a fool speak?
To prove to others that he is "wise."
He would be better off keeping quiet
    and fooling them, than opening his
    mouth and making a fool
    of himself.

Rabbi Nachman of Bratslav

Clowning is the wit of the fool.

Rabbi Menachem Mendel of Kotzk

Ten righteous people could have
    saved Sodom.
But all 1,000 fools can do is turn their
    leader himself into a fool.

Rabbi Menachem Mendel of Kotzk

It took at least ten righteous people
    to keep Sodom from
    being destroyed.
But all it would take is one fool
    to destroy the entire world.

Rabbi Levi Yitzchak of Berditchev

It takes a great deal of wisdom
  to prove to fools that there are wiser
  than they.

Rabbi Yechiel Michal of Alexander

Pretending to be amused when a
  fool tells a joke is also a kind
  of charity.

Rabbi Naftali of Ropshitz

I am not afraid of being sent to Hell.
I am afraid of being seated in Heaven
  next to a fool.

COMPASSION AND MERCY

Rabbi Chaim Halberstam of Tzanz

One who steers us clear of treacherous
    paths does us no less good
    than one who shows us the
    right way.

Rabbi Nachman of Bratslav

One must be merciful with mercy
    herself, because she is cast off by
    herself in a lonely corner
    and no one cares anymore to
    be merciful.

Rabbi Meir of Apta

Those who have no compassion for
    themselves have none for
    others either.

Rabbi Nachman of Bratslav

Ruler of the Universe:
Surely Your will is full of good
    and mercy.
But we have not the strength to receive
    such mercy.

Rabbi Asher of Stolin

Our mercy returns to us in kind—
    though it is about time
    that some of that mercy return to
    the Blessed Holy One!

Rabbi Moshe Leib of Sassov

When I am called to the afterworld
    I would prefer Hell over Heaven,
    because those who suffer
    are found there.

THE PIOUS AND
THEIR TEACHERS

Rabbi Menachem Mendel of Kotzk

Who can be called a pious person?
One who does not make what is
    primary, secondary, or does not
    make what is secondary, primary.

The Seer of Lublin

Pious people need to be like infants—
    happy and teary-eyed.
Happy because they are doing
    God's work.
Teary-eyed over their sins.

Rabbi Yaakov Shimshon of Shpitovke

> A pious person is one who mends
>   broken or cracked vessels,
>   returning them to their
>   former state.

Rabbi Menachem Mendel of Vorka

> A pious person is one who knows how
>   to fast while eating, and to be alone
>   in a crowd.

Rabbi Yisrael of Modzitz

> The Hebrew word *Hasid*, 'pious person,'
>   is the combination of the Hebrew
>   letter *yod* and the Hebrew word
>   *hesed*, "lovingkindness". That is to
>   show us that a *yod*, [meaning, *Yid*, a
>   Jew] who performs acts of *hesed*,
>   "lovingkindness", is a *Hasid*, a
>   pious person.

Rabbi Menachem Mendel of Kotzk

> A Hasid fears God.
> A Mitnaged fears the Shulkhan Arukh
>   [Code of Jewish Law].

Rabbi Menachem Mendel of Kotzk

There are Hasidim who can point to the
Heavens and say with full certainty:
"The Almighty is indeed God."

Rabbi Meir of Premishlan

"With the pious, you deal piously . . .
and with the perverse, you act
tortuously." (Psalms 18:26–27)
The key is in the company you keep.
If you are friends with the pious, then
you too shall be pious.
And if you are friends with the perverse,
then you too shall become twisted.

Rabbi Shneur Zalman of Liadi

The teachings of Kabbalah raise you to
the Heavens.
The teachings of Hasidism bring the
Heavens to you.

Rabbi David of Talne

They say I am a standard bearer.
The truth is, the only thing I bear is debt.

Rabbi Naftali of Ropshitz

A Prophet sees the future,
   and a Rabbi sees the present.
Sometimes it is more difficult to see the
   present, than it is to see the future.

Baal Shem Tov

By the power of my Prayer,
   I can transform this wooden table
   into gold.
But I would be embarrassed to pray to
   the Holy One for such a
   trivial thing.

Rabbi Yehuda Leib of Ger

I have no intention of playing the
   broker between merchants.
Rather, I intend to teach people to be
   good Jews.

Rabbi Yosef of Ishbitz

The Rabbi only raises the ladder.
The Jews must do the climbing on
   their own.

Rabbi Nachman of Bratslav

Like the number of threads in my Tallit
prayer shawl, so was the number of
tears that I cried until I could finally
understand the true meaning of
the Tallit.

Rabbi Nachman of Bratslav

When the Days of Awe come to an end,
I put my ear to the wall
to listen for the beadle's gavel,
hammering out its call for Selichot
services in the coming year.

The Seer of Lublin

"Righteous is God in all ways, and pious
[*Hasid*] in all works." (Psalms
145:17)
The righteous must worship God in all
His ways—
But the Hasid must worship God with
all His works—even in
material ways.

Rabbi Pinchas of Koretz

When I was young, I had to sit behind
the stove when I studied the Torah.
Nevertheless, I felt complete.
But now that I sit at the head of the
table when I study, I find I cannot
grasp the words' meaning.

Rabbi Menachem Mendel of Vitebsk

I discovered people in torn clothing
who nevertheless had hearts that
were intact.
But I strove to turn things around:
to dress them in fine clothing
and tear their hearts.

Rabbi Shlomo of Karlin

When the Hasidim are judged in the
Heavenly Court, all the forests and
fields through which they traveled
to visit their Rebbe, will be added
on as weight to the scale of their
good deeds.

Rabbi Uri of Strelisk

King David, of blessed memory, was
     able to compose beautiful Psalms.
And what am I able to do?
I am able to recite the Psalms.

Rabbi Tzvi Hersch of Romanov

I was taught the trade of the tailor—
     and I learned to put it to good use—
     careful to fix what was old—
     and not to ruin what was new.

GOOD AND EVIL

Rabbi Nachman of Bratslav

If you believe it can be broken,
then know it can also be fixed.

Rabbi Aharon of Karlin

Whoever does not rise in spirituality
descends in spirituality.

Rabbi Menachem Schneerson

The defeat of evil
in human battles
brings victory over evil
beyond humans as well.

Baal Shem Tov

> Just as the sweeper who cleans the
> courtyard gets dirtied himself,
> so can one who seeks to repair the
> world be contaminated by evil.

Baal Shem Tov

> Ever since the day that Esav duped his
> father Yitzchak, not a single
> righteous father may find fault in
> his son.

Rabbi Dov Ber of Mezritch

> In every evil, there is good.
> In every judgment, there is mercy.

Baal Shem Tov

> "Turn from Evil and do Good."
>   (Psalms 34:15)
> This means: Turn Evil into Good,
>   because Evil is the raw material
>   of Good.

THE MISSION
OF THE JEW

Baal Shem Tov

Every Jew comes into this world
    to fulfill some sort of calling.

Rabbi Moshe Teitelbaum

How did I become a Jew?
My rabbi and teacher took my soul out
    from my body to launder it
    in the same way that a launderer
    cleans a linen: by scrubbing it in a
    stream, scouring, washing, and
    drying it.
And, once it was purified,
    he returned it to me.

The Holy Jew

It is no great feat to be a miracle worker.
However, it is to be a Jew.

Rabbi Menachem Mendel of Vorka

There are three things that please
    the Jew:
Bowing erectly—
Shouting silently—
And dancing without moving.

Rabbi Yechiel Michal of Zlotchov

I bind myself to the entire
    Jewish People:
To those who are greater than I—to be
    uplifted, to those who are less than
    I—so they can raise themselves
    along with me.

Rabbi Moshe of Kobrin

If I knew that upon my arrival in
    Heaven they would say:
"A Jew has arrived,"
    I would have no worries at all.

Rabbi Mordechai of Lechovitz

A Jew is like a golden coin.
If at times it gets rusty or mired,
all you have to do is wash and scour
it and its luster will return.

Rabbi Chanoch Henich of Alexander

Jews who do not dance with joy
over the fact that they are Jews,
lack gratitude to Heaven.
They evidently have never heard
the blessing:
"Thank you, God, for not making me
a heathen."

Rabbi Shneur Zalman of Liadi

An abundance of awe towards God
is hidden in every Jew's intuition.

Rabbi Moshe of Kobrin

God does not lack for angels.
What is needed are healthy and
wholehearted Jews who can carry
out God's will.

Rabbi Yechiel Meir of Gustinin

People can sit and study the Torah and
    pray for seventy years,
    but if they lack sincerity,
    then in the end they will not have
    become one iota of a real Jew.

Rabbi Mordechai of Lechovitz

Jews who do not totally devote
    themselves are no Jews.

Rabbi Yechiel Meir Lifschitz

It is easy to appreciate the value of
    precious stones and pearls.
But it is quite difficult to understand
    even the smallest bit of what it
    means to be a Jew.

Rabbi Nachman of Bratslav

A Jew, no matter how far he falls,
    because he is who he is,
    always remains hopeful
    of repenting and returning to the
    Blessed One!

Rabbi Avraham Mordechai of Ger

> Even the pouch that holds the tefillin
>   is holy.
> If it falls to the ground, even by mistake,
>   you must pick it up immediately
>   and kiss it.
> And a Jew who puts on those tefillin,
> How much more is that person holy!

Baal Shem Tov

> There is no such thing as a lonely Jew.
> Wherever there is a Jew, there too
>   is God.

Rabbi Mordechai Yosef Leiner of Ishbitz

> Every Jew who falls,
>   falls into the lap of God.

Rabbi David of Lelov

> There is no such thing as evil Jews,
>   because if you look at the evil
>   within them you will discover that
>   that part is not Jewish at all.

Rabbi Menachem Mendel Schneerson

". . . who in great mercy revives the
    dead." (from the Amidah prayer)
One must emulate God in this respect.
That is why every Jew must strive to
    "revive the dead"— that is, to instill
    liveliness and vitality in every
    Jew's life.
It is like resuscitating a dead body with
    living spirit.

Rabbi David Forkes

The Sovereign of the Universe said:
Were it not for the sins of the People of
    Israel, whence would I receive
    Confession that is so sweet?
Whence would I hear an "Ashamnu"
    ["We have sinned"] filled with
    such Passion?

Rabbi Yehoshua of Kutnah

"This is the ritual of the guilt offering.
    It is most holy." (Leviticus 7:1)
Even the guilty sinner of Israel
    is most holy.

Rabbi Yisrael of Rizhin

One should never despair of any Jew.
Even the wickedest Jew retains some
grasp of Judaism.
After all, a bucket that tumbles into a
well can still be pulled from the
depths if it is attached to a rope—
whether a thick one or a thin one.

Rabbi Menachem Mendel of Kotzk

"Your descendants shall be strangers in
a land not their own."
(Genesis 15:13)
The Jews are better off as strangers in
exile, in a land not their own,
than always trying to pander to
their neighbors in order to achieve
citizenship with equal rights.

Rabbi Simcha Bunam of Pshis'cha

"And Yaakov sent messengers ahead to
Esav his brother." (Genesis 32:4)
When a Jew is being chased by "Esav,"—
that is, in their hour of need—
they may even trouble the divine
messengers on high for help.

Rabbi Aharon of Karlin

"Israel encamped there in front of the
    mountain." (Exodus 19:2)
Wherever Jews camp,
    a mountain stands in front of them.

Rabbi Yitzchak of Vorka

"Israel encamped there in front of the
    mountain." (Exodus 19:2)
All Israelites found favor with
    their neighbors, and thus did
    they merit receiving the
    Ten Commandments.[1]

Rabbi Aharon of Karlin

God said: "You shall be for Me a
    treasured possession."
    (Exodus 19:5)
The very fact that "You shall be
    for Me," makes them a
    "treasured possession."

---

1. Play on Hebrew root *chen*, meaning "to camp"
and "to find favor."

Rabbi David of Lelov

God said: "You shall be for Me a
    treasured possession [Hebrew:
    segulah]." (Exodus 19:5)
They shall be like the *segol* [a triangular
    Hebrew vowel symbol], which, no
    matter how you turn it, always
    remains a triangle.
Such is the nature of Jews:
No matter how you twist or turn them,
    they always remain Jews.

Rabbi Menachem Mendel of Kotzk

A whole non-Jew is better than
    a half-Jew.

Rabbi Meir Margalit of Austra

A heathen riots because things are too
    good for him, a Jew because they
    are too bad.

Rabbi Levi Yitzchak of Berditchev

Just as we are in awe of You,
    so will the heathens be in awe of us.

Rabbi Levi Yitzchak of Berditchev

Even we, the Jews, do not fulfill God's
    will—how much less so
    the heathens.

Rabbi Chaim Yechiel of Sompolna

It is true that we have brought on
    miracles, but the heathens have
    brought on even greater miracles:
The abyss dividing Heaven and Earth
    has grown larger and deeper.

Passions

Rabbi Naftali of Ropshitz

Where are our human urges found?
Wherever we believe they are absent.

Rabbi Dov Ber of Mezritch

A person is slave to two Rulers:
One's Deity and one's desires.

Rabbi Tzvi Elimelech of Dinov

If any possibility of the Evil Impulse
acting in the name of the Good
Impulse were eliminated—many
indecent acts could be prevented.

Rabbi Nachman of Bratslav

Human urges are similar to a person
    walking with a clenched fist.
One deludes others into believing that
    there is something in the hand,
    but when it is open, they find that
    there is nothing there after all.

Rabbi David of Lelov

The Evil Impulse can often drive people
    to do good deeds.
But as the people's zeal grows,
    they find they have destroyed
    everything in their path.

Rabbi Mordechai of Chernobyl

The Evil Impulse promises immediate
    gratification.
Not so the Good Impulse, which acts
    much more slowly, as in the
    Talmudic phrase: "The good deed
    today, its rewards tomorrow."
    (Talmud, *Eruvin* 22a)
That is why people are so attracted to
    the Evil Impulse, because of its
    instantaneous payoff.

Rabbi Mordechai of Neshkiz

You may be asleep, but your Evil
Impulse is wide awake.

Baal Shem Tov

One can learn a great deal by observing
the Evil Impulse—for example, the
great lengths it will go to achieve
its purpose.
Now you, on the other hand, do only the
absolute minimum.

Rabbi Mordechai of Chernobyl

This is why the Evil Impulse is called
"The Instigator":
Not only does it provoke people to turn
from the straight path, but it also
taunts them when it is done, saying
"Look how far you have strayed!"

Rabbi Nachman of Bratslav

The Evil Impulse looms large among
scholars, to induce them to invent
whole new sets of restrictions.

Rabbi Dov Ber of Radoshitz

It would never occur to anyone that the
Evil Inclination can appear in the
guise of a venerable old man with
beard, sidelocks, and a holy
countenance, full of zeal for
the Creator.

Rabbi Nachman of Bratslav

It is enormously difficult for the
Evil Impulse to lead the entire
world astray.
That is why he plants a phony "famous
Rebbe" here and there, to mislead
people in large groups.

Baal Shem Tov

A clever merchant lets the customers
first taste for free—but afterwards,
they pay an arm and a leg for the
merchandise.
That is exactly how the Evil
Impulse works.

Rabbi Leibele Eger

Angels have no evil inclination.
Humans do.
Nevertheless, by overcoming their evil
      inclination, humans can rise to a
      greatness beyond that of angels.

Rabbi Yehiel Michal of Zlotchov

Just as the Evil Impulse tries to entice
      humans to sin, so does it try to
      entice them to be overly righteous.

Rabbi Chaim Meir Yechiel of Magelnitze

The Evil Impulse can tempt us into
      fasting for three days straight—
      just so that we gorge ourselves
      afterwards!

Rabbi Nachman of Bratslav

To what are humans' thoughts similar?
To a clock pendulum,
      which swings toward both sides,
      good and evil, without discerning
      between them.

Rabbi Mendel of Romanov

There are two types of Evil Impulses:
one that incites people to sin,
and the second that convinces them
afterwards that what they have
done is a good deed.

Baal Shem Tov

When the Evil Impulse finds that no
one is paying it any attention,
it poses as the Good Impulse, and
causes people to engage in feigned
acts of kindness.

Rabbi Aryeh Leib, the Grandfather of Shpoli

Every generation must find new
methods to fight the Evil Impulse,
because he becomes familiar with
the old methods, and he knows how
to defeat them.

Rabbi Menachem Mendel of Kotzk

There are times when the Evil Impulse
latches on to people by means of
their tears.

Rabbi Leibele Eger

There is no one as smart and as clever,
as devious and as cunning, as the
Evil Impulse.
So why is it they call it a fool?
Because it deals with fools.

Rabbi Menachem Mendel of Gustinin

A peg can be hammered into the wall
only because the hammer is
stronger than it.
If people get swept away into a
whirlpool of sin it is only because
they foolishly listen to their
weaker impulses.

Rav Moshe Chaim of Sadilkov

There are fools who are kidnapped by
the Evil Impulse and thrown into
his sack.
They continue on, though they are his
prisoners, still believing that none
are as righteous as they, though
they remain wrapped in his bag.

Rabbi Simcha Bunam of Pshis'cha

The Evil Impulse must be viewed as a
murderer, standing before you with
an ax, ready at any moment to cut
off your head.
If it is hard for you to envision him
thus, that is a sign he has already
cut off your head!

Rabbi Nachum of Chernobyl

Both Yaakov and Esav can be found in
all people.

Rabbi Yechiel of Mosh

Ruler of the Universe:
Yours is a wonderful people.
Sinners?
Take away the Evil Impulse for one day
and You shall see what precious
Jews there are in Your world.

DREAD OF SIN

Rabbi Menachem Mendel of Vitebsk

True fear of sin:
To be afraid of the sin itself, even more
than of the punishment that comes
in its train.

Rabbi Menachem Mendel of Kotzk

I wish that people would avoid sin not
because it is forbidden, but because
they do not have the free time to
waste on sin.

Rabbi Menachem Mendel of Kotzk

Instead of adding severity to the law,
it would be better to add the fear of
God to its performance.

Baal Shem Tov

Sin and its delights are also derived
from the Heavenly pleasures.

FEAR OF GOD

Rabbi Aharon of Karlin

> Awe without love is imperfect.
> Love without awe is worthless.

Rabbi Menachem Mendel of Kotzk

> When a year is blessed,
>   it is blessed with all things—
>   even with the fear of God.

177

ANGER

Rabbi Nachman of Bratslav

One must sweeten anger with
compassion.

Rabbi Pinchas of Koretz

For many years I wrestled with my
    Anger, until finally I conquered him
    and placed him in my pocket.
Now I take him out only when I
    need him.
But I am so angry with him, that I do
    not ever want to take him out again!

Rabbi Menachem Mendel of Lubavitch

> Wrath is one of the greatest sins—
> > so much so that even if one finds it
> > entirely necessary to get angry
> > one must still seek permission—
> > much as one must seek permission
> > to marry an abandoned wife.[1]

Rabbi Nachman of Bratslav

> Children become fools when their
> > parents are quick-tempered.

Rabbi Raphael of Bershad

> Anger poisons both the inside and
> > the outside:
> It destroys the soul.

---

1. In Jewish law, one must get Rabbinical permission to marry a woman who has not been formally divorced.

The Author and the Book

Rabbi Nachman of Bratslav

> A righteous person can learn much
> about authors' souls from what they
> have authored.

Rabbi Menachem Mendel of Lubavitch

> One speaks to the masses, writes for a
> whole generation, and publishes for
> generations to come.

Rabbi Nachman of Bratslav

> A likeness of the author is imprinted in
> every book.

THE HEART

Rabbi Menachem Mendel of Kotzk

A broken heart is a whole heart.
A leaning ladder is a straight ladder.

Rabbi Nachman of Bratslav

Those who are pure-hearted
        can tell the future by listening to
        their hearts:
Because the core of godliness lies within
        the heart, and thus, what the heart
        utters are the words of the
        living God.

Rabbi Yosef Asher Zelig of Strikov

> Those who are heartbroken are upset
>   with themselves.
> Those consumed with sorrow are upset
>   with others.

Rabbi Menachem Mendel of Kotzk

> "Words from the heart are taken to
>   heart." (Rabbi Moshe Ibn Ezra,
>   *Shirat Yisrael*)
> —Including the heart from which the
>   words come.

SONG AND SPEECH

Rabbi Moshe of Kobrin

A song is like a parable.
One has to understand its deeper
spiritual meaning, to fathom
its application.

Rabbi Levi Yitzchak of Berditchev

Songs and hymns are the work of
lyricists and poets.
But only after they have been drenched
with Jewish tears, do they become
prayers and petitions.

Rabbi Shneur Zalman of Liadi

> Speech is the pen of the heart.
> Music is the pen of the soul.

Rabbi Nachman of Bratslav

> A translation can be good and bad.
> Sometimes it transcends, and
>   sometimes it transgresses.

HUMAN QUALITIES

Rabbi Yisrael of Rizhin

So you want to break some of your
old habits?
You will break your back first.

Rabbi Menachem Mendel of Kotzk

"Some day I will do it"—is self-deceptive.
"I want to do it"—is weak.
"I am doing it"—that is the right way.

Rabbi Nachman of Bratslav

Heroes are seldom also wise.

Rabbi Levi Yitzchak of Berditchev

Stalking sin and pursuing good are
     admirable quests.
But be sure to look for sin in yourself
     and for good in others.

Rabbi Dov Ber of Mezritch

This is how one must rule over one's
     moral qualities:
To learn how to be proud—and not
     be proud.
To learn how to be angry—and not
     be angry.
To learn how to speak—and to
     remain quiet.
To learn how to be quiet—and to speak.

Rabbi Yaakov Yosef of Polnoye

Flattery is worse than idolatry.

Rabbi Menachem Mendel of Rimanov

Humans are born with enormous
     deficiencies in order that they can
     make up for them.

Rabbi Menachem Mendel of Rimanov

Buffoonery can destroy the
whole world.
If Pharaoh had understood the power of
buffoonery he would never have let
the Israelite People out of Egypt.
He would have simply strewn jocularity
among them and gotten rid of them
through their own foolish quips.

Rabbi Menachem Mendel of Kotzk

Habit is dangerous.
It creeps up surreptitiously like a thief.

LESSONS FROM
EVERY SOURCE

Rabbi Simcha Bunam of Pshis'cha

From chess we learn several things:
People must always act with
    great caution.
They must weigh their every step.
And they must think seventy-seven
    times before making a move.

Rabbi Aharon Rokeach of Belz

One can learn a useful lesson from
    everything.
What can one learn from a taxi?
    Humility.
When you get in, you have to lower your
    head and bend your knees.

Rabbi Moshe Leib of Sassov

I learned three things from observing
an infant:
—Never sit idle, not even for a moment.
—When asking something of your father,
burst out immediately in tears.
—Once your needs have been fulfilled,
fill yourself with joy and forget
your sadness.

Rabbi Dov Ber of Mezritch

This is what I learned from a thief:
He is willing to do the brunt of his work
even at night.
If he does not get what he set out for that
night, he does not despair, he just
goes out and gets it another night.
He and his mates love each other deeply
and completely.
He dedicates himself wholeheartedly,
even to something of little value.
He attaches little value to what he does
get, selling it for half its worth the
following day.
He finds his craft most appealing and
would not give it up for another.
He endures countless pains and blows
but is not offended.

Rabbi Avraham Yaakov of Sadigora

You can learn something from
everything:
From the railways we learn that one
moment's delay can throw
everything off schedule.
From the telegraph we learn that every
word counts.
And from the telephone, that what we
say here, they hear there.

Rabbi Leibele Eger

I learned three things in Kotzk:
—That humans are humans, and
angels are angels.
—That if one wants, one can be even
greater than an angel.
—"In the beginning, God created...,"
means that God created just the
beginning—and left the rest for us
to complete.

Money

Rabbi Meir of Apta

You cannot really love money, because
money cannot love you back.
It just goes from one pocket to the next.
People simply covet money, and that is
why they are never satisfied.

Rabbi Nachman of Bratslav

Those addicted to avarice die penniless
and debt-ridden.

Rabbi Gershon Hanokh of Radzin

Even those who shun ill-gotten profit
can be bribed.

Rabbi Moshe of Lelov

God commanded the Israelite people
    to borrow golden and silver objects
    from the Egyptians (Exodus 12:35)
    so that they would always be afraid
    to return to Egypt because of
    their debts.

Rabbi Moshe of Kobrin

"Save me from blood-guilt, God."
    (Psalms 51:16)
What King David, the author of the
    Psalms, meant was:
Keep me, my God, from ever
    worshipping Mammon, the blood-
    stained god of money.[1]

Rabbi Nachman of Bratslav

All forms of idolatry are somehow
    connected with money.

---

1. Play on Hebrew *damim*, which means both
"blood" and "money."

Rabbi Meir of Premishlan

"Wrap up the money in your hand. . . ."
    (Deuteronomy 14:25)

Keep your money under wraps, in your
    hand, so that you can keep control
    over it, and so that it does not,
    Heaven forbid, take control
    over you.

DEEDS AND ACTIONS

Rabbi Moshe of Boyan

How can people be responsible for their
own actions when they do not even
have authority over themselves?

Rabbi Moshe of Kobrin

"The essence of wisdom is the fear
of God.
All who practice it gain sound
understanding." (Psalms 111:10)
From this verse we learn that gaining
sound understanding is not
dependent on a person's wisdom,
but on one's practice [deeds].

Rabbi Yisrael of Rizhin

What is forbidden is forbidden.
But what is permitted—do not rush off
to do anyway.

Rabbi Shalom Dov Ber of Lubavitch

Better one deed than a thousand sighs.

Rabbi Nachman of Bratslav

If people truly believed with a complete
faith that God could provide them
with all their needs, they would
never take a single trip, ever.

GOOD DEEDS AND SINS

Rabbi Leibele Eger

Preparing to do a good deed is more
important than doing the good
deed itself.

Rabbi Elazar Halevi Ish Horvitz

Awe and love are the wings of
good deeds.

Rabbi Shneur Zalman of Liadi

An infinite light is hidden in every
good deed.

Rabbi Aharon of Karlin

Righteous people are those who
    constantly wait for the opportunity
    to do good, so that they can utilize it.

Rabbi Pinchas of Koretz

There are people who are brought to
    this world to live up to seventy
    years, in order to do only one
    mitzvah properly.

Rabbi Naftali of Ropshitz

The brothers Shimon and Levi zealously
    pursued Heavenly deeds.
Yet Yaakov still said of them: "Cursed be
    their anger." (Genesis 49:7)

Rabbi Mordechai of Lechovitz

If only hedonists knew about the great
    pleasures that good deeds bring,
    they would dedicate themselves
    to the fulfillment of Torah
    and mitzvot.

Rabbi Avraham Yaakov of Sadigora

We are commanded to drink wine on
  certain occasions.
And yet, as in any commandment, we
  must make sure not to overdo it.

Rabbi Yitzchak Meir of Ger

The pages of the Torah are filled with
  stories—of sin and more sin.
From these stories about sinning came
  much of the Torah.
Who knows what might emerge
  from our performance of
  God's commands?

Rabbi Elimelech of Lizhensk

I am very suspicious of minor
  transgressions, which are
  considered less severe.
When you stick a needle into the flesh
  of living beings, it will pierce them
  and cause great pain.
But if you prod them with a thicker rod,
  it does not hurt as much.

Rabbi Menachem Mendel of Kotzk

"And you shall live by them [God's
  Laws]" (Leviticus 18:5)
The phrase "live by them" means:
Perform them with liveliness
  and enthusiasm.

Rabbi Nachum of Chernobyl

I am more concerned about the good
  deeds that I did with satisfaction,
  than I am about the sins that I
  committed without satisfaction.

Rabbi Menachem Mendel of Kotzk

There are those who perform good
  deeds in public and sin in secret.
And there are those who sin in public
  and do good deeds secretly.

Rabbi Moshe Yitzchak of Pshevorsk

When one commits a sin, the rejoicing
  comes before the act.
When one performs a good deed, the
  rejoicing comes after the act.

Rabbi Moshe HaKohen of Razvadov

Sometimes one hears about another
person's sin, and has more pleasure
in knowing about it than the one
who does the sin. In such a case
what difference does it make who
committed the sin, since both of
them take pleasure from it.

Rabbi Yehuda Aryeh Leib of Ger

Just as having sinful thoughts is more
severe than sinning, having good
thoughts is more important than
doing good deeds.

Baal Shem Tov

Even in sin there are sparks of light,
which repentance can cause to
shoot forth.

Rabbi Zussya of Anapoli

An evil spirit is created from every sin.
But a whole evil spirit has never been
created from a Jewish sin, because
no Jew ever sins with a whole heart.

Rabbi Dov Ber of Mezritch

"Sinful thoughts are more severe than sinning itself." (Talmud, *Yoma* 29)
If one has sinful thoughts it is a sign that one has already committed a sin, because without sin there is no such thought.

MELANCHOLIA

The Seer of Lublin

I have nothing but praise for a
 contented ignoramus who does not
 know how to do anything but pray.
He is far happier than the
 melancholy scholar.

Rabbi Mordechai of Lechovitz

In the World-to-Come the Blessed
 Holy One will exact punishment
 from those who wrap themselves in
 a Tallit of depression, and call
 it piety.

Rabbi Mordechai of Lechovitz

Melancholia is no melody,
     neither in this world nor in the next.

Baal Shem Tov

Fear of God without joy
     is not fear at all, but melancholia.

Baal Shem Tov

"They could not drink the water of
     marah ['Bitterness'], because it was
     bitter." (Exodus 15:23)
Meaning: They themselves were bitter,
     which is why they tasted bitterness
     in the water.

MUSIC

Rabbi Nachman of Bratslav

Tears open gates.
Music demolishes walls.

Rabbi Yisrael Taub of Modzhitz

They say that the Temple of Music is
near the Palace of Repentance.
But I say it is one and the same place.

Rabbi Yisrael Taub of Modzhitz

When I hear a Jew chanting a melody
I can tell how deep runs this Jew's
fear of God.

Rabbi Nachman of Bratslav

One can tell whether a person has
accepted the yoke of Heaven
by the sound of their song.

Rabbi Nachman of Bratslav

There is nothing that does not have its
own tune.
Even heresy has its own melody.

Rabbi Chaim of Tzanz

There are those who do not get their
music from the Heavenly Palace
of Song, but only from the
musical notes.

SECRETS

Rabbi Menachem Mendel of Kotzk

Wherever there is a secret there
is stealing.

Rabbi Shmuel Schneerson

There are three different levels of
people with secrets:
The first: You can tell they have a secret,
but they still do not reveal it.
The second: You cannot even tell that
they have a secret.
The third: Even if you tell them their
own secret, they still act as if they do
not know a thing about it.

211

Rabbi Menachem Mendel of Kotzk

> If we find that we have to conceal
> something and keep it a secret,
> it means that we are doing
> something wrong.

Rabbi Simcha Bunam of Pshis'cha

> A secret is something that you
> pronounce in a way that everyone
> hears but no one understands.

TALES AND STORIES

Rabbi Nachman of Bratslav

It is said that stories can help put you to
sleep.
I say stories can help wake you up.

Rabbi Nachman of Bratslav

There is nothing that restores the soul,
purifies the heart, deepens the
mind, and brings one closer to our
Father in Heaven, than a story of
heroic deeds.
Come and see: the Blessed Holy One
relates the stories of Genesis first,
before spelling out all of the laws of
the Torah.

Rabbi Shalom Dov Ber of Lubavitch

> You need to be smart to know how to
>   tell a story properly.
> But you need to be even smarter
>   to know how to listen to a
>   story properly.

Baal Shem Tov

> When the Hasidim gather to tell stories
>   about the righteous,
> God looks upon it as if they were
>   learning about *Ma-aseh Merkavah*
>   [deep mystical doctrines].

WORSHIP

Rabbi Shalom Dov Ber of Lubavitch

Worship begins with the words "I
thank You."[1]

"The Holy Jew" of Pshis'cha

There are no rules when it comes to
worshipping God—including
this one.

---

1. Note: "I thank You, Ruler of the Universe!" are
the first words of the first morning prayer in Jewish
liturgy.

Rabbi Yaakov of Porissov

Not only is one who worships God truly
devoted.
So is one who *desires* to worship God.

Rabbi Menachem Mendel of Kotzk

I would never want to worship a God
whose ways are comprehensible to
every simple mortal.

Rabbi Ze'ev Wolf of Z'barazh

One should be jealous even of idle
revelers, who learn how to stay up
all night.
In the next world, they will be able to
worship God day and night.

Rabbi Menachem Mendel of Kotzk

There is nothing more purifying than a
stream of water.
However, when such a stream is frozen,
you can carve an idolatrous image
upon it.

The Seer of Lublin

What do you do when there is no ritual
   bath in the area?
You immerse yourself in a river of fire
   with the flame of devotion.

Rabbi Menachem Mendel of Kotzk

When you stand on the bottom rung of
   a ladder, you check to see if it is
   sturdy and strong, and only then
   do you proceed to climb to the
   next rung.
Such is the way of the worshipper.
You must proceed step by step, rung
   by rung.

Rabbi Simcha Bunam of Pshis'cha

"And you must love Adonai your
   God with all your heart. . . ."
   (Deuteronomy 6:5)
These words are directed towards *you*.
One who attempts to worship God with
   another's heart is nothing better
   than an idol worshipper.

THIS WORLD AND THE NEXT WORLD

Rabbi Nachman of Bratslav

> All of the desires of this world are like
>   rays of light.
> You try to catch them in your hand
>   only to find there is nothing in
>   your grasp.

Rabbi Yehoshua of Ostrovtsa

> If only people knew how far this world
>   was from being theirs, there would
>   be no more bewilderment
>   or confusion.

Rabbi Shneur Zalman of Liadi

This world is the least of all worlds.
And yet, at the same time, it is greater
than any other.

Rabbi Baruch of Medzibuz

How easy and simple this world of ours
can be if only we do not give in
to idleness.
And how dark and difficult it can be
if we do.

Rabbi Yechezkel of Kozmir

People in this world are like those
walking on ice:
Running is out of the question—lest
they slip.
Dancing, by the same token, is even
less advisable.
Taking small steps is also unwise—lest
the ice melt before they make
it across.
The only rule is: just go ahead and cross!

Rabbi Nachman of Bratslav

One must cross this world on a very
    narrow bridge.
But the main thing to recall:
Have no fear at all.

Rabbi Wolf of Strikov

You are not as good as you think,
    nor is the world as bad as you think.

Rabbi Elazar of Poltosk

I would love, just once, to get a glimpse
    of the future for which so many
    people toil.

Rabbi Yehuda Aryeh Leib of Ger

I wish I were a bird, which has no "this
    world" nor the "next."

Rabbi Naftali of Ropshitz

The only way to get to the World-to-
    Come is through this world!

Rabbi Simcha Bunam of Pshis'cha

People should prepare two passages
    for themselves:
One to exit this world, and the other, to
    enter the next.

Baal Shem Tov

Though the stars above seem like tiny
    dots of light, they are actually
    entire worlds.
Such are the people in this world who
    seem lowly and plain:
They will be great in Heaven.

Rabbi David of Mikoleib

When I return from a fair, my
    children ask:
What did you bring back for us?
When I return from the fair of life,
    They will ask me on High:
What did you bring back for us?
What shall I answer?

Baal Shem Tov

Accept everything that happens to you
　　in this world with love.
That way, you shall gain both this world
　　and the next.

UPS AND DOWNS

Rabbi Leib of Kovel

Those who fail always lay the blame on
    the obstacles in their path:
On the potholes in the road,
    on the shoes on their feet.
But they themselves . . . . well, they have
    always behaved impeccably, and are
    completely blameless.

Rabbi David of Mikoleib

When you rise up to bless the
    Torah—it is the Torah that should
    be raised up, by you.

Rabbi Moshe of Kobrin

When you go through the furrows of a
        field you must go up and down
        from one flower bed to the next.
This is true as well when you
        worship God.
At times you ascend and at times
        you descend.
At times you overcome your base
        impulses, and at times they strike
        back at you.
Just make sure that you strike the
        final blow.

Rabbi Elimelech of Kozhnitz

There are those who ascend
        but have no idea that they are aloft.
They actually think that the ground
        has fallen from underneath them.

Baal Shem Tov

A constant delight becomes habitual
        and loses its pleasure.
That is why worship has its high points
        and its lows—so that it always
        remains a pleasure.

Rabbi Menachem Mendel of Kotzk

Horses walk in the middle of the road,
not men.

Rabbi Yitzchak Zelig of Sokolov

In the past, people would ascend to the
Heavens while their bodies
continued traversing the earth.
Now, people are falling into the abyss,
while their bodies ascend
to Heaven.

Rabbi Nachman of Bratslav

Sometimes "ups and downs" are really
just "ups."
Because the whole point of going
"down" is so that you can grow
stronger, and start over again, to
replenish your mind, restore your
vitality, and renew your life.

Rabbi Nachman of Bratslav

Even when they have fallen into deep
mud, some people know only how
to scream and scream and scream.

Rabbi Dov Ber of Mezritch

Sometimes you have to rake through
many ashes to find one
glowing ember.

Rabbi Shlomo of Karlin

If you want to pull someone out of the
mire, it is not enough to stand
above them with an
outstretched hand.
You yourself have to climb into the
muck, immersing yourself fully in
the mud.
Only then can you grasp them with
both hands and pull them out
with you.

HUMILITY AND ARROGANCE

Rabbi Menachem Mendel of Kotzk

All moral qualities require a certain
    degree of intent—except
    for humility.
Because intentional humility
    cannot qualify as humility.

Rabbi Noah of Lechovitz

If I have a debt of money, I borrow from
    one person to pay another.
Why do I need honor? I do not have a
    debt of honor to anyone.

Rabbi Pinchas of Koretz

> Disingenuous humility is better than a
> genuine condemnation.

Rabbi Shalom Rokeach of Belz

> There are two types of humble people:
> Those who see themselves as worthless
>   and the whole world as worthless—
>   their humility is imperfect.
> But those who view the world as worthy
>   but themselves as worthless—now
>   theirs is a perfect humility.

Rabbi Moshe of Yadner

> Idolatry's heretic is called a Jew.
> Pride's heretic is called pious.

Rabbi Avraham of Slonim

> Giving in to those greater than you
>   is easy.
> Giving in to those beneath you is
>   also easy.
> That is what is called being humble.
> But it is very hard to give in to a
>   colleague who is your equal.

Rabbi Nachman of Bratslav

No one depends on people more than
someone who is seeking glory.

Rabbi Raphael of Bershad

One who receives honor is not as great
as one who bestows it, because the
former is a taker.
And a taker is always lower than
the giver.

Rabbi Moshe of Lelov

Lowly horse, oh how I envy you.
How many pure souls do you delight!

Rabbi Yisrael of Rizhin

There is no ascetic like the horse.
It eats hay, sleeps on the ground, its
eyes are closed, it has nails in its
feet, it does not demand honor of
anyone, nor does it chase
after power.
Yet, despite all this, it's just a horse,
and no one is required to give
it honor.

Rabbi Dov Ber of Mezritch

Fire? One finds fire in ashes.
If you search for fire on mountaintops
    you will find only wind, you will
    reap only gusts.

Rabbi Yechezkel of Kozmir

Why do we bless God on the fringes of
    the Tallit and not on the Tallit itself?
Because the fringes hang down, and are
    dragged along the ground humbly
    and abjectly.
That is why they are most important.

The Seer of Lublin

People who truly humble themselves
    are guaranteed never to go wrong.
They wrong neither themselves
    nor others.

Rabbi Yitzchak Meir of Ger

No quality is greater than lowliness,
    except to bear someone who
    flaunts it.

Rabbi Noah of Lechovitz

> The clock is the king of modesty
> and humility.
> Indeed, it declares:
> Another hour has gone by and what
> have I fixed in this world?

Rabbi Levi Yitzchak of Berditchev

> What good is a world like this, which
> suffers one so lowly as I?

Rabbi Pinchas of Koretz

> All that begins modestly ends
> in greatness.
> But that which does not begin modestly
> cannot end in greatness.

Rabbi Moshe Leib of Sassov

> When one person teaches another,
> it is like pouring from one vessel to
> a second.
> But for that to happen, the receiving
> vessel must be lower.

Rabbi Aharon II of Karlin

Those who are lowly are on their
way up.
And those who are on their way up
are lowly.

The Seer of Lublin

People who are worthless, but who are
aware of their worthlessness, are
better than virtuous people who are
aware of their virtue.

Rabbi Barukh of Stutshik

Whoever does not try to grab a place,
has a place in every place.

Rabbi Menachem Mendel of Kotzk

Those who worship themselves
are guilty of idolatry.

Rabbi Tzvi of Rimanov

When does one begin to be haughty?
When one begins to relish one's honor.

Rabbi Yisrael of Plotsk

> Pride and Modesty must be
>   like garments:
> Sometimes you put them on and
>   sometimes you take them off.
> But you should not have them simply
>   for the sake of having them.

Rabbi Wolf of Zhitomir

> One must learn about humility from
>   pride itself, for what is more
>   humble and simple than pride?
> It is found among the lowest and basest
>   of human beings, and wherever
>   there are empty and ignorant
>   people—it befriends them.

Rabbi Yehoshua of Ostrovtsa

> Liars are preferable to the arrogant.
> At least liars do not believe their
>   own lies.
> The arrogant believe their own
>   deceptive fantasies and even take
>   pride in them.

Rabbi Avraham of Porissov

There is no one as misguided as
    the arrogant.
They still believe in their own
    self-importance even as everyone
    else is mocking them.

Rabbi Chaim of Karsenah

It is difficult to perceive pride with
    the eye.
It is easier to smell it with the nose.
This is in contrast to a lit candelabrum:
If you look at it, you absorb light.
If you smell it, you absorb smoke.

Rabbi Pinchas of Koretz

Every sin requires some sort of action:
Raising your hand, moving your feet,
    curling your lip.
Except for pride.
A person needs only to lie back, yawn,
    and say to oneself:
I am great.

Rabbi Noah of Lechovitz

How strange are the ways of humanity.
If one eats an apple with its peel, one is
    called a glutton.
If one eats the apple without it, one
    seems haughty.

Baal Shem Tov

The source of all sadness is pride.
The proud person thinks he is entitled
    to everything.

Rabbi Simcha Bunam of Pshis'cha

There are "loners" who remove
    themselves from society, but still
    peek out from the crevices of their
    hiding place to see if others are
    confused and wondering from afar
    about their disappearance.

Rabbi Levi Yitzchak of Berditchev

There is only one permitted boast:
"My patron is God on High!"

Rabbi Tsadok HaKohen of Lublin

Pride does not necessarily involve
    insolence or overt condescension.
It is possible simply to feel proud
    just within oneself.

Rabbi Simcha Bunam of Pshis'cha

Even a chimney sweep, who comes out
    of the chimney black from head to
    toe, boasts to himself, as everyone
    takes a step away:
"I am the greatest chimney sweep in the
    world. There is none greater."

Rabbi Raphael of Bershad

The arrogant are prone to say:
I am smart, I am rich, I am learned,
    I am righteous, I am kind, I am
    honest, How humble am I, I, I, I . . .

Rabbi Hillel Moshe of Bialystok

I will not fatten my arrogance
    with fasts.

Rabbi Levi Yitzchak of Berditchev

If pride were not mentioned in
    the Torah, I would not believe that
    you could find such a trait among
    human beings.
Constructed entirely from clay, I cannot
    imagine how they can boast so.
And they—their whole lives a passing
    shadow—like a potsherd that
    shatters one day alive, the
    next dead.

Rabbi Menachem Mendel of Kotzk

Pride is a flaw.
But the proud—even when they are
    brought to the depths of humility
    by Heaven itself—still cling to
    their pride.

Rabbi Menachem Mendel of Kotzk

Utterly righteous people who have
    never tasted sin are also worthy of
    mercy—lest they grow proud of
    their righteousness and become
    arrogant, which is the severest
    of sins.

Rabbi Menachem Mendel of Kotzk

> Even when you get rid of all of your
>   lustful desires, the Evil Impulse still
>   manages to entice you to
>   act arrogantly.

Rabbi Simcha Bunam of Pshis'cha

> It is written: "As a face reflects its face in
>   water, So does one's heart to
>   another." (Proverbs 27:19)
> Why in water? Why not in a mirror?
> Because to see one's own face in the
>   water one has to bend down.
> Not so with a mirror.
> With a mirror one can remain upright
>   and erect.

Rabbi Shmelke of Nikolsburg

> "You shall cherish your neighbor's
>   honor as you do your own."
>   (Mishnah, *Avot* 2:15)
> Meaning: You should cherish the
>   respect your neighbor gives you as
>   you cherish your own self-respect.
> If you have none of the latter, then you
>   shall not have any of the former.

Rabbi Yitzchak Eizik of Komarna

You should always be honest and fair,
   but should never act self-righteously
   or be overly pious, because that is
   the material of arrogance, which
   itself is sewn from the threads of
   sorrow and indifference.

Baal Shem Tov

"It threw truth to the ground . . . ."
   (Daniel 8:12)
Truth is the signature of the Holy One,
   like a shining gem that rests
   underground, undisturbed by
   human hands.
One cannot extract this gem from the
   ground without first bending down.
Yet no one is willing to lower himself!

Rabbi Menachem Mendel of Kotzk

"They stood crowded together, yet they
   bow comfortably" (Mishnah,
   Avot 5:5)
When they stand haughtily, with their
   backs erect—it seems crowded.
Yet when they bow humbly—it
   becomes spacious.

Rabbi Nachman of Bratslav

The Messiah will not come until all
arrogance has been done away with.

POVERTY AND WEALTH

Rabbi Moshe of Kozhnitz

When people are paupers, they do not
    blame their failure on themselves.
They complain to the Ruler of
    the Universe.
But the wealthy boast and brag:
"Through my own strength and might
    have I accomplished this."
    (Deuteronomy 8:17)

Rabbi Elimelech of Lizhensk

Poor people with their meager rations
    can get caught up in gluttony more
    easily than rich people with their
    heaping portions.

Rabbi Menachem Mendel of Kotzk

> I fear neither poverty nor hunger.
> Both are gifts from God.
> What I fear is the callousness and the
>   cruelty that often afflict
>   the hungry.

Rabbi Ze'ev Wolf of Strikov

> I envy the poor.
> They toil in vain, but they do not suffer
>   in vain.
> Because their suffering leads them
>   to Heaven.
> But what can you do? The poor still
>   envy the rich.

Rabbi Dov Ber of Radoshitz

> The worst thing about poverty is that
>   the poor person believes that wealth
>   will remove suffering.

Rabbi Yehezkel of Shinova

> How pitiful is the miser, who lives with
>   poverty in order to die with wealth.

Rabbi Aryeh Leib, the Grandfather of Shpoli

Paupers ask for money to live on—so, in
actuality, what they are really
begging for is life.
The wealthy tend to live for their
money—so, in actuality, what they
are really begging for is money.

Rabbi Yissachar of Volborzh

The poor person and the rich person,
are both hungry.
With the single difference that the poor
person is saddened by hunger,
and the rich person rejoices in it.

Rabbi Moshe of Makarov

Only arid ground can become saturated
with water.
Wet earth will only turn to mud.
Likewise, only the poor need money to
become revitalized.
The wealthy turn their money into mud
and sink into it until they drown.

Rabbi Shlomo of Radomsk

> Sometimes even the wealthy are to
>   be envied:
> With every penny they give away, the
>   recipient drags them one step closer
>   to Heaven.

Rabbi Simcha Bunam of Pshis'cha

> Wealth is like salt:
> It makes our food savory—but the more
>   one drinks salty water, the thirstier
>   one gets.

Rabbi Yitzchak Meir of Ger

> If the Messiah were meant to arrive on a
>   fancy chariot, instead of riding on a
>   donkey, then all wealthy persons
>   would fancy themselves
>   the Messiah.

ADVICE

Rabbi Pinchas of Koretz

Usually, persons asking for advice
have already solved their own
problem without knowing it.

Rabbi Nachman of Bratslav

It is easier to give advice to others
than to oneself.

SLOTH

Rabbi Yitzchak Meir of Ger

So-and-so does not labor to seek a
     livelihood.
He says he has great trust in God,
     but in truth, he is merely lazy.

Rabbi Menachem Mendel of Kotzk

Temperate people make their way
     deliberately, and thus they do not
     rush into anything.
Idle people are too lazy to act
     deliberately and therefore their
     behavior is rash.

249

Rabbi Yitzchak Meir of Ger

Heathens love to come to blows.
It is in their nature to strike.
And they especially enjoy hitting Jews.
But, thankfully, they are lazy.

LIVELIHOOD

Rabbi Simcha Bunam of Pshis'cha

It is easy for me to understand how a
person without income is able
to survive.
For such a one survives by Faith and
Trust in God.
But what I do not understand is:
How does a person who has ample
income survive?

Rabbi Levi Yitzchak of Berditchev

Jews are so worried about making a
living that they forget they must
fear God as well.

251

Rabbi Menachem Mendel of Kotzk

"You shall eat dust all the days of your
    life." (Genesis 3:14)
What kind of curse is this?
Indeed, this curse guarantees that the
    snake will be well fed wherever it
    goes, without having to worry the
    least bit about it.
But perhaps that is exactly what makes
    this curse so poignant.
It is as if God were saying:
I do not want anything to do with you.
I do not even want to feed you.

Rabbi Meir of Premishlan

"God will battle for you, and you may
    remain still." (Exodus 14:14)
Indeed, it is God who provides everyone
    with bread, but one still must go out
    and plow.[1]

---

1. Plays on Hebrew roots *lacham*, which means
both "to battle" and "bread," and *cheresh*, which means
both "to be still, silent" and "to plow."

The Seer of Lublin

> "Human sustenance is as difficult to
> attain as splitting the Red Sea."
> (Talmud, *Pesachim* 118a)

Just as the splitting of the Red Sea was
an unexpected miracle, similarly,
our sustenance comes from an
unexpected place.

THE RIGHTEOUS AND THE WICKED

Rabbi Levi Yitzchak of Berditchev

Who is righteous?
One who seeks to right all wrongs
    before God.

Rabbi Simcha Bunam of Pshis'cha

"And God saw that Leah was unloved."
    (Genesis 29:31)
Yaakov did not hate her, Heaven forbid.
It was Leah who hated herself.
Such is the way of the righteous—they
    only see their own flaws and
    shortcomings and cannot
    tolerate themselves.

255

Rabbi Nachman of Bratslav

The righteous are the masters of
the world.

Rabbi Yisrael of Rizhin

The righteous sow the world with seeds
of light.
Whose fault is it that people shield their
eyes from the gentle radiance?

Rabbi Mordechai of Neshkiz

Any Zaddik who does not feel the labor
pains of every woman within fifty
miles, and pray for her, does not
deserve to be called a *Zaddik*.

Rabbi Moshe of Kobrin

The righteous behold the World-
to-Come.
But as for this world—they only hear
about it.
The simple see this world, but only hear
about the World-to-Come.

Rabbi Uri of Strelisk

It is worth it to travel a thousand miles,
neglecting study and prayer, just to
hear one utterance of truth from a
person of truth.

Rabbi Chaim of Tzanz

The urge to be righteous is an urge like
all other urges.
But in order to fulfill it, you must first
get rid of all urges.

Rabbi Naftali of Ropshitz

The righteous are always angry at
themselves, full of rage at their
very existence.
Why? Because they believe they will
never live up to their
own expectations.

Rabbi Nachman of Bratslav

The righteous are permitted to break
down other people's gates in order
to clear their path.

Rabbi Dov Ber of Mezritch

"Seven times the righteous person
stumbles and yet rises again."
(Proverbs 24:16)
It is important for a righteous person to
fall down seven times, because after
each fall, the righteous person
discovers some sparks of insight on
the way up.

Rabbi Levi Yitzchak of Berditchev

"I am Adonai your God." (Exodus 20:2)
God said to Moshe:
I am your God, do with me as you wish.
Because the righteous decree, and God
fulfills their will.

Rabbi Simcha Bunam of Pshis'cha

"God gives sight to the blind, God
straightens those who are bent, God
loves the righteous." (Psalms 146:8)
Why are the righteous grouped together
with the physically impaired here?
Because there is no such thing as a
handicapped righteous person who
believes that he is righteous.

Rabbi Yaakov Yosef of Polnoye

The deeds of the evil ones are the
starting point of deeds of
the righteous.

The Seer of Lublin

Righteous people must not love
themselves.
Evil people ought to hate themselves.

Rabbi Pinchas of Koretz

In order to love an evil person who is
not totally evil, it is sufficient to be a
righteous person who is not
totally righteous.
But to love a wicked person who is
totally wicked, it is necessary to be
a righteous person who is
totally righteous.

Rabbi Moshe of Razvadov

One who does not fear lightning and
thunder is either completely
righteous or completely wicked.

Rabbi Levi Yitzchak of Berditchev

What is the difference between the
   righteous and the wicked?
The righteous seem low in their
   own eyes.
The wicked seem low in others' eyes.

The Seer of Lublin

I prefer a wicked person who knows he
   is wicked, to a righteous person
   who knows he is righteous.

Rabbi Tzadok HaKohen of Lublin

Just as the wicked will stand trial
   for ruining the world with their
   evil, there are those who will stand
   trial for ruining the world with
   their righteousness.

Rabbi Menachem Mendel of Kotzk

Those who sin and pardon themselves
   are worse than those who are
   completely wicked.

Rabbi Naftali of Ropshitz

"The wicked, even at the gates of Hell,
  do not repent their evil ways."
  (Talmud, *Eruvin* 19a)
They will not confess their guilt
  because they believe they have done
  nothing but good deeds.

The Seer of Lublin

"The wicked, even at the gates of Hell,
  do not repent their evil ways."
  (Talmud, *Eruvin* 19a)
They are convinced they are being led to
  Hell only to redeem the poor souls
  that are already there.

Rabbi Menachem Mendel of Kotzk

Esav was no clumsy peasant dressed in
  fancy garments (cf. Genesis 25:28)
  who walked around barefoot and
  tended his pigs.
Esav had a long beard and sidelocks.
He was the leader of a great clan, who
  would recite the Torah at the Third
  Shabbat Meal.
But nevertheless . . .

Rabbi Chaim of Tzanz

I searched the entire Torah and yet I
never found a single commandment
requiring us to execute evil people
and bury them.
And yet there are those who search
throughout the world for any victim
to bury.
And when they cannot find a righteous
person, then they make do with a
wicked one.

Rabbi Menachem Mendel of Kotzk

As wicked as Pharaoh was, at least he
was a man!
He endured ten harsh plagues, and still
stood his ground.
Today's skeptics are fleas.[1]
When a single arrow hits their heel,
immediately they collapse and
are helpless.

---

1. Play on Hebrew *Par'o*, "Pharaoh", and *par'osh*,
"flea".

Rabbi Menachem Mendel of Kotzk

"Let the wicked give up their ways . . . ."
(Isaiah 55:7)
What ways? The wicked have nothing
but mud.
The verse means: Let the wicked give up
the way that they consider a way,
but is really no way at all!

CHARITY

Rabbi Zussya of Anapoli

When collecting charity be sure to take
along two pouches: one to collect
abuse and complaints, and the other
to carry the coins.

Baal Shem Tov

Good deeds done in self-interest and not
for their own sake are better off not
being done at all.
Except for charity.
The poor gain benefit from charity
regardless of its source.

Rabbi Menachem Mendel of Kotzk

> When our ancestors were wandering in
>   the desert, eating manna from
>   Heaven, everyone received an equal
>   portion of food: one measure
>   per head.
> So how were they able to fulfill the
>   commandment of giving charity?
> Our ancestors contributed knowledge
>   for charity.
> The learned gave charity to those
>   less knowledgeable.

Rabbi Nachum of Chernobyl

> Money that has not been sanctified
>   by removing the proper amount for
>   charity, can be compared to meat
>   that is unsalted:
> It stinks!

Rabbi Dov of Liaba

> When the poor come to you and tell you
>   that they do not have food for
>   Shabbat, and you deign to wrap
>   yourself in faith and tell them to
>   trust in God—that is true heresy.

Rabbi Zvi Elimelekh of Dinov

Conventional wisdom considers it a sin
to give disreputable people even a
few measly coins of charity, and a
praiseworthy act to grind them
into dirt.

I prefer to commit such a "sin," and to
forego the "reward" of that
praiseworthy act.

Rabbi Ze'ev of Strikov

"Do not rob the poor man because he is
poor." (Proverbs 22:22)

The meaning of this verse is this:

If you do not want to contribute charity,
then don't.

But do not steal from the poor man his
status of poverty, by telling him he
is not deserving of charity.

STINGINESS

Rabbi Simcha Bunam of Pshis'cha

The Torah neither forbids stinginess,
    nor condemns it.
That is because stinginess is a disgrace
    and there is no need to condemn
    something that is
    already contemptible.

Rabbi Yitzchak Meir of Ger

Sinners are better than misers.
When sinners sin, they regret it.
But misers sin and enjoy it—because
    they get to keep their money.

Rabbi Yitzchak Zelig of Sokolov

A miser is worse than a thief:
The eye of the thief is fixed on what he
    does not have.
But the eye of the miser is fixed on what
    he has and also on what he does
    not have.

Rabbi Menachem Mendel of Kotzk

For the miser, the only world is the
    World-to-Come.
Indeed, he does not derive the slightest
    bit of pleasure from his wealth.
Where, then, for him is *this* world?

Rabbi Yehezkiel of Shinova

How pitiful is the miser:
He lives with poverty in order to die
    with wealth.

Jealousy and Greed

Rabbi Menachem Mendel of Kotzk

Jealousy and greed come from two
    different sources:
People are born with jealousy,
    but greed is nurtured.

Rabbi Moshe of Kossov

The desire to pray in front of the
    congregation is the most
    contemptible of all desires.
At least people indulge their other
    desires with a measure of modesty.
But this one—the more people who
    listen, the more the desire grows.

Rabbi Chanoch Henich of Alexander

Greedy? For what?
Jealous? Of what?
Honor? For what?

Rabbi Yehoshua of Ostrovtsa

Why envy what you do not have,
    when what you do have is not really
    yours anyway?

Rabbi Yaakov Yosef of Polnoye

Just as there are those greedy for
    material goods, there are those
    greedy for spirituality as well.

Rabbi Pinchas of Koretz

When one grows old, although one's
    physical strength weakens, one's
    impulse of greed does not, because,
    despite the infirmity of old age, one's
    force of habit only grows greater.

Rabbi Nachman of Bratslav

The essence of adultery is in one's gaze.

Rabbi Aharon of Karlin

It is possible for one to fast from
Shabbat to Shabbat—and still be
a glutton.

"The Holy Jew" of Pshis'cha

When the evil urges abandon the
elderly because they are old and
their strength has waned—they are
like those who have overcome
their greed.

Rabbi Levi Yitzchak of Berditchev

There are those who only love their
wives carnally, thus fulfilling
their lust.
The truth is that they do not really love
their wives at all—just themselves.

Rabbi Nachman of Bratslav

Adulterous lust is strong enough to
drive you crazy—indeed, you would
have to be crazy to engage in it.

DANCE

Baal Shem Tov

A dance before the Blessed Holy One
is prayer.

Rabbi Nachman of Bratslav

One must dance each and every day
—whether in thought or in action.

Rabbi Aharon of Karlin

The power of dance is so great that it
lifts you high above the ground.

Baal Shem Tov

The angel Michael makes a crown
out of the sandals that fell off of
Jews' feet as they danced on
the holidays.

SHABBAT AND FESTIVALS

Rabbi Baruch of Medzibuz

I would be willing to give up my place
in the World-to-Come in order to
observe the Shabbat properly.
Indeed, Shabbat transcends even the
World-to-Come.

Rabbi Baruch of Medzibuz

Shabbat is greater than the
World-to-Come.
Indeed, Shabbat is the spring
from which the World-to-Come
was drawn.

Rabbi Shneur Zalman of Liadi

The holy light of Shabbat and festivals
  shines even in the souls of
  the ignorant.

Rabbi Avraham Yehoshua Heschel of Apta

If I could, I would cancel all of the fast
  days save the Day of Atonement
  and the Ninth of Av, which
  commemorates the destruction of
  the Temple.
After all, on the Day of Atonement, who
  needs to eat?
And on the Ninth of Av, who can eat?

Rabbi Uri of Strelisk

When the Days of Awe, the great days of
  repentance and spiritual
  reawakening, are over, our souls are
  liable to leave our bodies out of
  their zealous desire to serve God.
But the Holy One is filled with
  compassion for us, and commands
  us to take refuge in the Sukkah.

Rabbi Simcha Bunam of Pshis'cha

The duty of sitting in the Sukkah
is a considerable one.
After all, one must enter it in one's
entirety: one's whole body, all of
one's limbs, one's clothes—
even one's shoes.

Rabbi Menachem Mendel of Kotzk

"The person who is in discomfort is not
obligated to dwell in the Sukkah."
(Sukkah 26a)
A Jew who sits in the Sukkah and is
made uncomfortable by the rain,
was not worthy of sitting in the
Sukkah to begin with.

PEACE

Rabbi Nachman of Bratslav

The crux of peace is in combining
two opposites.

Rabbi Nachman of Bratslav

There are famous scholars whose fame
comes only as the result of
a dispute.

The Seer of Lublin

A deceptive peace is better than a
true war.

Rabbi Nachman of Bratslav

Every day we draw nearer to our
    dying day.
Who has time to quarrel?

HAPPINESS AND SADNESS

Rabbi Nachman of Bratslav

The essence of happiness lies in
the heart.
But the heart cannot rejoice until all of
its crookedness is removed.

Rabbi Aharon of Karlin

Sorrow is no sin, and neither is joy a
good deed.
But no sin can cause the foolishness that
sorrow causes, and no good deed
can bring you to the places that
happiness can.

Rabbi Tsadok HaKohen of Lublin

Joy is the key to wealth.
Even if one has as much money as there
    are grains of sand, if one has no joy,
    one is poor.

Rabbi Dov Ber of Mezritch

Happiness without conviction
    is debauchery.

Rabbi Yisrael of Rizhin

I suspect that even crooks are welcomed
    into Heaven, because their days are
    filled with happiness.

The Baal Shem Tov

One who lives in happiness fulfills the
    will of God.

Rabbi Nachman of Bratslav

One should root out all grief and woe,
    and plant them within happiness
    and joy.

Rabbi Pinchas of Koretz

Every pleasure comes directly from
Heaven—even jokes and quips—
but only if they are told out of
honest joy.

Rabbi Moshe Leib of Sassov

A perpetual pleasure is no pleasure
at all.

Rabbi Shlomo Leib of Lentshno

". . . If God gives me bread to eat and
clothes to wear . . . ." (Genesis 28:20)
Ruler of the Universe, give the children
of Israel bread so that they can
eat cheerfully.
Because when people are ill or
miserable they have no appetite.
And give them clothes to wear
without the misery of needing to
pawn it because of poverty.

Rabbi Aharon of Karlin

There is a thin line between sadness
and bitterness.

Rabbi Aharon of Karlin

The happiness of a simple person is
more important than the happiness
of a sad Hasid.

Rabbi Aharon of Karlin

Even the best kind of bitterness is
tinged by sadness.
And even the worst kind of happiness
is drawn from a holy spring.

Rabbi Aharon of Karlin

The meaning of sorrow: I am owed, I
am in need—everything for one's
own benefit, nothing for the sake
of Heaven.
Who says you are owed and that you are
not indebted to others?

Baal Shem Tov

Sorrow locks the gates of Heaven.
Prayer opens locked gates.
Joy has the power to tear down
the walls.

Rabbi Simcha Bunam of Pshis'cha

"May all who seek God rejoice."
    (I Chronicles 16:10)
Human nature dictates that all who
    search for a lost object are troubled,
    and only after they find it do
    they rejoice.
But those who seek God are steeped in
    joy, even during the search.

Rabbi Shneur Zalman of Liadi

A broken heart is not the same
    as sadness.
Sadness occurs when the heart is stone-
    cold and lifeless.
On the contrary, there is an
    unbelievable amount of vitality
    in a broken heart.

The Seer of Lublin

Sadness that comes from sinning is
    worse than the sin itself, because
    the sufferer becomes depressed and
    has no heart to serve God.

Study of Torah

Rabbi Nachman of Bratslav

> Torah, without good deeds, is like a
> myrtle leaf—it smells sweet but has
> no taste.

Rabbi Menachem Mendel of Kotzk

> The plain and simple meaning of the
> Torah is the secret of the Torah.

Rabbi Menachem Mendel of Kotzk

> You say you study the Torah.
> But what does the Torah teach you?

Baal Shem Tov

Why does the Torah begin with the
    second letter of the Hebrew
    alphabet, *bet* [rather than the first
    letter, *alef*]?
To show you that you do not even know
    the first thing about it.

Rabbi Menachem Mendel of Kotzk

A teacher of the young is greater even
    than his master, because his master
    teaches things that he interprets one
    way—and then others come along
    and contradict him, interpreting
    them another way.
But the teacher of the young says
    nothing but the plain and
    simple truth.
After all, everyone agrees that an *alef* is
    an *alef* and a *bet* a *bet*.

Rabbi Yitzchak Meir of Ger

Being a teacher is a
    worthwhile endeavor.
That way you may find a good student,
    and learn a few things yourself.

Rabbi Yisrael of Rizhin

There are times when one should teach
　　Torah in public for the sake of one
　　specific person.
And there are times when one should
　　refrain from teaching Torah in
　　public, for the sake of one
　　specific person.

Rabbi Menachem Mendel of Kotzk

Some people recite words of Torah
　　to reach the seventh Heaven.
I think one should recite the Torah
　　to reach the center of the listener.

Rabbi Menachem Mendel of Kotzk

Shavuot, the Feast of Weeks, is called
　　"The Time of the *Giving* of
　　the Torah."
Why is it not called "The Time of the
　　Receiving of the Torah"?
Because the Torah was given to
　　everyone in equal measure, but
　　everyone chooses to receive it
　　according to their wisdom and their
　　capacity to understand.

Rabbi Menachem Mendel of Kotzk

Why is food so expensive?
Because everyone consumes food.
When everyone is consumed with Torah
    study, then Torah study will be
    expensive and food cheap.

Rabbi Elimelech of Lizhensk

The Torah was handed down to us in
    fire, so that we would know to
    uphold it with burning passion
    and commitment.

Rabbi Shabtai of Roshkov

One must uphold the commandment:
"You shall be fruitful and multiply,"
        with regard to Torah study as well,
        so that the mind does not become
        sterile and barren.

Baal Shem Tov

"God's teaching is completely
        perfect. . . ." (Psalms 19:8)
No matter how much you turn it,
        it remains perfect and complete.

Rabbi Yehoshua of Ostrovtsa

> One does not need idle disputes to
>   straighten out matters in the Torah.
> They were not bent in the first place.
> The truth is not a wooden board
>   whose knots need straightening.
> After all, one who straightens a ladder,
>   only bends it.
> And one who bends a bow, only
>   straightens it.

Rabbi Menachem Mendel of Kotzk

> "It [the Torah] is not in the Heavens."
>   (Deuteronomy 30:12)
> The Torah does not belong to those
>   who believe they have reached the
>   highest Heavens.

PRAYER

Rabbi Aryeh Leib, the Grandfather of Shpoli

One who prays without feeling is like
  one who piles up heaps of sand,
  plaster, and bricks, but has no water.
How does one expect to cement
  them together?

Rabbi Mordechai of Lechovitz

Every word of a prayer needs to be
  chanted from the depths of the soul.
If one mistakenly skips a word and says,
  "Universe" instead of "Ruler," for
  example, then the prayer was not
  recited properly.

Rabbi Yaakov Yosef of Polnoye

It is easier for one to come up with five
new insights into the Torah than it
is to recite one prayer with
deep feeling.

Rabbi Shneur Zalman of Liadi

Prayer without devotion is like a body
without a soul.

Rabbi Shneur Zalman of Liadi

Prayer needs to be continuous like
a thread.
The slightest fray and the thread
unravels and tears.

Rabbi Chaim Halberstam of Tzanz

Before I begin to recite my prayers,
I pray to be able to pray.

Rabbi Menachem Mendel of Kotzk

The person who prays today merely
because he prayed yesterday, is
worse than a sinner.

Rabbi Uri of Strelisk

Who ever said that one must pray with a
whole heart?
Perhaps it is preferable to pray with a
broken heart?

Rabbi Pinchas of Koretz

Everyone believes that one prays before
the Blessed Holy One.
But it is not so.
Prayer *itself* is the essence of Divinity.

Rabbi Chanoch Henich of Alexander

I am in the habit of removing one
prayer from the service, so that it
does not become habitual.
But I am afraid that that too will
become habitual.

Rabbi Pinchas of Koretz

If you hear about a man whose teeth fell
out of his mouth as he was praying,
because he trembled so much
before God—know that it was I.

Rabbi Menachem Mendel of Kotzk

> If you do not have a four-cornered
>   Tallit, then wrap yourself in the
>   four corners of the world, and pray.

Baal Shem Tov

> "Go into the ark, you and your whole
>   household. . . ." (Genesis 7:1)
> You must put your whole heart and
>   mind into every word you speak.[1]

---

1. Play on Hebrew *tayvah*, meaning both "ark"
and "word."

The Exaltation
of Repentance

Rabbi Menachem Mendel of Kotzk

If I were told that I could never atone
for my ways, then if I had to overturn
Heaven and Earth to do so, I would.

Rabbi Simcha Bunam of Pshis'cha

People are not to blame for the fact that
they sin.
Indeed, they withstand great temptation
though their strength is negligible.
They are, however, to blame for the fact
that they do not repent their evil
ways, because they always have the
ability to do so.

Rabbi Baruch of Medzibuz

Ruler of the Universe:
Is it really necessary to suppress Your
people until they are utterly
dejected, and then ask them to
atone for their ways?
Allow them some leeway, and some
peace of mind, and then ask them
to repent.
Then their repentance will be sincere!

Rabbi Menachem Mendel of Kotzk

It is enough to open your heart the
smallest amount—even the width of
a pin head—to repent, so that you
feel a prick in your heart, like a
piercing sting in living tissue, not
like a needle thrust into dead flesh.

Rabbi Yisrael, the Maggid of Kozhnitz

"Return, O Israelites, to Adonai your
God." (Hosea 14:2)
This verse means: One must return to
the place where the Adonai is *your*
God; that is, to the divinity that is
within you.

Rabbi Menachem Mendel of Vitebsk

There are moments in the life of the
worst reprobate of being closer to
the Blessed One than a perfect saint.
When?
During moments of Repentance.

Rabbi Dov Ber of Mezritch

Just as oil is stowed within the olive,
so is penance stowed within the sin.

Rabbi Shalman Zalman of Kapost

When one repents, it is not always
necessarily over sin.

Rabbi Shmelke of Nikolsburg

If I had the choice, I would rather
not die.
Because in the World-to-Come there are
no Days of Awe, and what can a
person's soul do without the
Day of Atonement?
What is the point of living
without Repentance?

Rabbi Simcha Bunam of Pshis'cha

On the Day of Atonement, we say, "We
    are guilty," and saying so, we think:
God will be happy to forgive us!
And when we say, "We have acted
    treacherously," we think:
Once God pardons us, all will be well!
However, in this case, neither was
    confession made nor
    penitence done.

INDEX OF BIBLICAL VERSES

INDEX TO PASSAGES FROM PIRKE AVOT

INDEX OF NAMES

About the Editor

Simcha Raz was born in Jerusalem and is a prominent educator and author. His rabbinical ordination is from Merkaz HaRav Kook Yeshivah in Jerusalem. He is the author of numerous books on Jewish lore and hasidic spiritual wisdom, many of which have been translated into English. He has received several literary prizes and hosts literary media programs in Israel. This book is translated from his Hebrew collection, *Pitgamay Hasidim* (*Hasidic Sayings*), published in 1981.

About the Translators

Dov Peretz Elkins is an internationally known author, lecturer, and educator. His pioneering books on experiential learning, values clarification, and spirituality have influenced a generation of rabbis, educators, and Jewish communal service workers. His most recent books include: *Prescription for a Long and Happy Life, Moments of Transcendence: Inspirational Readings for Rosh Hashanah and Yom Kippur*, and *Jewish Guided Imagery*. He is currently the spiritual leader of The Jewish Center, in Princeton, New Jersey.

Jonathan Elkins was born in Augusta, Georgia, and grew up in Rochester, New York. He has been living in Tel Aviv for the past several years, where he works as a freelance writer and television reporter and commentator. He has degrees in literature and philosophy from the University of Pennsylvania, and in Near Eastern and Judaic studies from Brandeis University.